Stories on Board!

Stories on Board!

Creating Board Games from Favorite Tales

Dianne de Las Casas

Illustrated by Soleil Lisette

 LIBRARIES UNLIMITED

AN IMPRINT OF ABC-CLIO, LLC
Santa Barbara, California • Denver, Colorado • Oxford, England

Library of Congress Cataloging-in-Publication Data

De Las Casas, Dianne.
    Stories on board! : creating board games from favorite tales / Dianne de Las Casas ; illustrated by Soleil Lisette.
        p. cm.
    Includes bibliographical references.
    ISBN 978-1-59158-862-7 (hard copy : alk. paper)—ISBN 978-1-59158-864-1 (ebook)
1. Board games.   2. Fairy tales.   3. Games.   I. Lisette, Soleil.   II. Title.
    GV1312.D44   2010
    794—dc22   2010007232

ISBN: 978-1-59158-862-7
EISBN: 978-1-59158-864-1

14   13   12   11   10   1   2   3   4   5

This book is also available on the World Wide Web as an eBook.
Visit www.abc-clio.com for details.

Libraries Unlimited
An Imprint of ABC-CLIO, LLC

ABC-CLIO, LLC
130 Cremona Drive, P.O. Box 1911
Santa Barbara, California 93116-1911

This book is printed on acid-free paper ∞

Manufactured in the United States of America

For my dear friend, Meinard Cruz,
Whose passion for books
helps teachers promote literacy
throughout the Philippines.
Maraming salamat po!
–Dianne de Las Casas

For Nana and Paw Paw.
Thank you for your neverending
love and support!
–Soleil Lisette

Contents

Stories

Introduction

My work in storytelling has led me to become a teaching artist in the classroom. In my school residencies, I work for an extended period with the students, teaching them storytelling techniques. The residency often culminates in a group activity. With *Stories on Board!*, it culminates in a "Game Day."

I grew up playing board games. I love how board games not only bring people together in a spirit of fun competition, it also allows people to spend time together, sharing both chagrin and laughter as the game pieces move around the board.

One day, as I was rewriting a favorite folktale, the idea hit me. I could combine my favorite folktales and my love of board games into a fun, educational method that encompassed reading, writing, math, and social studies. *Stories on Board!* was born. On a chilly, windy day in February at Pensacola Beach, Florida, I was inspired and furiously typed out the method on my laptop.

Meinard Cruz from Scholastic Book Fairs Philippines has been a longtime client and, now, friend. He asked me to come to the Philippines and give workshops to teachers there. I was delighted when he agreed to let me debut *Stories on Board!* with the teachers in the Philippines. The workshop was a smash hit. The teachers LOVED the technique and are now using the method with their students.

I used the technique in a two-week residency at one of my favorite schools in Louisiana—Bissonet Plaza Elementary. The students LOVED the fun they were having creating the board games. The teachers loved how much instruction and learning was involved. Game Day was done during P. E. time and the P. E. teachers loved it so much they asked to keep several of the student-created games to use on rainy days.

I am amazed by the creativity and teamwork I witness when students create their board games using the Stories on Board! method. They have a sense of pride because they create their own game. Surprisingly, many of the students I work with have never even played a board game! It is a pleasure to see students laugh and encourage each other during the games.

Since then, I have taught this method in professional development workshops and in schools across the country. Thank you to the countless teachers and librarians who understand the educational value of board games.

Stories are . . . fun and games! Let's play!

Warmly,
Dianne de Las Casas
dianne@storyconnection.net
www.storyconnection.net

The *Stories on Board!* Process

A Brief History of Board Games

A board game is played on a flat surface called a game board. Board games are believed to have been around for more than 4,000 years. "The Royal Game of Ur," which was discovered around 1926 by Sir Leonard Woolley in royal tombs of what is now Iraq, dates back to more than 2500 BC. It is believed to be the oldest complete board game ever found. Board games have been discovered in African, Asian, ancient Greek, and ancient Roman cultures.

Board games have two basic types of play: strategy and racing. The objective of strategy games is to capture or block opposing pieces and control the game board. The objective of racing games is to begin at a starting point and race along to a finishing point. There are board games that have both characteristics. The games that the students create in the *Stories on Board!* technique are racing games.

Introduction to *Stories on Board!*

Stories on Board! is a great way to introduce a unit on folktales, covering language arts and social studies. With *Stories on Board!*, students read and listen to popular folktales, analyze the structure of the story through story mapping, and then create a board game based on their analysis. It is an effective way to address students with multiple learning styles: aural learners, visual learners, and tactile learners. In this

1

lesson, students hear the story (aural), create the game board (visual), and play the game (tactile). The lesson culminates in a Game Day in which the students play each others' games.

Meeting Benchmarks Using the *Stories on Board!* Method

The following benchmarks are taken from the Standards for the English Language Arts by the National Council for the Teachers of English and the International Reading Association. Using *Stories on Board!* in the classroom allows students to meet these language arts benchmarks:

- Students read a wide range of print and nonprint texts to build an understanding of texts, of themselves, and of the cultures of the United States and the world; to acquire new information; to respond to the needs and demands of society and the workplace; and for personal fulfillment. Among these texts are fiction and nonfiction, classic and contemporary works.

- Students apply a wide range of strategies to comprehend, interpret, evaluate, and appreciate texts. They draw on their prior experience, their interactions with other readers and writers, their knowledge of word meaning and of other texts, their word identification strategies, and their understanding of textual features (e.g., sound-letter correspondence, sentence structure, context, graphics).

- Students adjust their use of spoken, written, and visual language (e.g., conventions, style, vocabulary) to communicate effectively with a variety of audiences and for different purposes.

- Students apply knowledge of language structure, language conventions (e.g., spelling and punctuation), media techniques, figurative language, and genre to create, critique, and discuss print and nonprint texts.

- Students develop an understanding of and respect for diversity in language use, patterns, and dialects across cultures, ethnic groups, geographic regions, and social roles.

- Students participate as knowledgeable, reflective, creative, and critical members of a variety of literacy communities.

- Students use spoken, written, and visual language to accomplish their own purposes (e.g., for learning, enjoyment, persuasion, and the exchange of information).

Warm-up

When beginning the lesson for *Stories on Board!*, start by telling a familiar folktale, which can then be discussed with the class. Together, the class can break down the story and create a story map, which will provide them with a framework from which to work when they analyze their own stories.

Game Playing with Grades K-2

With grades K-2, tell the story that accompanies the board game you plan to use ("The Gingerbread Jam," "The Little Red Hen's Pizza Party," etc.). If you decide to create your own board game, the game should be made with simple illustrations and spaces denoted with addition or subtraction signs. Students will need to be instructed that the plus sign (+) means to move forward; the minus sign (–) means to move back. Children may also need instruction on how to count the dots on the die, how to count the spaces, and how to move the pieces around the board. After a few practice runs, the students usually understand how to play.

Second graders playing "Gingerbread Jam" by Dianne de Las Casas based on the story "The Gingerbread Man."

First grade students playing "Pigopoly" by Dianne de Las Casas based on the story, "The Three Little Pigs."

First grade students play "The Little Red Hen's Pizza Party" based on "The Little Red Hen Makes Pizza" by Dianne de Las Casas.

Mapping Out the Story

To create the board game, the stories are mapped into the following:

- Main Characters
  - Characteristics of each character (antagonist, protagonist, helper)
  - Possible characteristics: good, evil, magical, etc.
- Main Characters' Motivations (what are their goals?)
  - Protagonist's motivation
  - Antagonist's motivation
  - Supporting character's motivation
- Story Perils (obstacles)
  - Peril 1
  - Peril 2
  - Peril 3
- Aids (elements in the story that aid the protagonist)
  - Aid 1
  - Aid 2
  - Aid 3
- Triumphs (overcoming obstacles)
  - Triumph 1
  - Triumph 2
  - Triumph 3

Some stories may have more than three perils, aids, and triumphs. In this case, students will have more choices when defining the spaces on their game boards. Be aware that some perils may not have a corresponding aid or triumph.

Vocabulary

- Main character—the characters in the story who have the largest role
- Supporting characters—characters in the story who have a minor role

- Protagonist—main character who is usually "good," the hero

- Antagonist—main character who is the protagonist's adversary

- Adversary—a person, group, or force that opposes or attacks; enemy; foe; an opponent in a contest

- Motivation—the goals of the characters in the story

- Peril—an obstacle in the story that prevents the protagonist from achieving his/her goal

- Triumph—the overcoming of the obstacle in the story

- Aids—elements in the story that aid the protagonist either through a third party or through the character's own devices

- Clockwise—moving from right to left in the direction of a clock's hands

Using the story map, have the students map out the preceding terms. Here is an example using the story, "Cinderella."

- Main Characters
  - Cinderella—protagonist
    - Characteristics—beautiful, kind, loving, loyal, hard-working
    - Motivation—to get to the Prince's ball
  - Stepmother and stepsisters—antagonists
    - Characteristics—mean, greedy, bullies
    - Motivation—to prevent Cinderella from attending the ball
  - Fairy Godmother—protagonist
    - Characteristics—caring, sympathetic, benevolent, magical
    - Motivation—to help Cinderella get to the ball

- Supporting Character
  - Prince Charming—protagonist
    - Characteristics—handsome, kind, determined
    - Motivation—to find a bride
    - Second motivation—to find Cinderella after the ball

- Story Perils, Aids and Triumphs Number 1
  - Peril—Cinderella doesn't have a dress
  - Aid—Fairy Godmother appears
  - Triumph—Cinderella receives a dress

- Story Perils, Aids and Triumphs Number 2
  - Peril—Cinderella doesn't have a way to get to the ball
  - Aid—Fairy Godmother turns pumpkin into a coach
  - Triumph—Cinderella has a ride to the ball
- Story Perils, Aids and Triumphs Number 3
  - Peril—Cinderella loses glass slipper
  - Aid—Cinderella gets to keep the matching slipper
  - Triumph—The prince finds Cinderella and both slippers fit

Individual and Group Work

Individual Work

Students can be assigned a story to work on individually. With this method, the individual student maps out his story and creates his own game board. A student's work can be assessed with the Stories on Board! rubric.

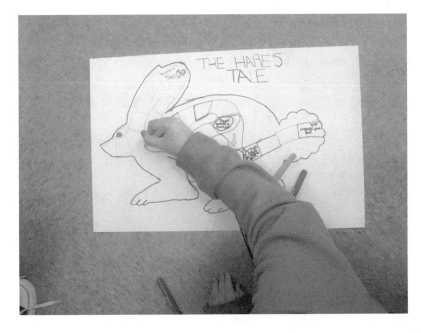

A third-grade student works on "The Hare's Tale" based on the story, "The Tortoise and the Hare."

Group Work

In this method, students work in groups of four to six, creating a group board game. Each student has to contribute a peril and a triumph to define spaces on the board game. The students' work can be evaluated with the Stories on Board! rubric.

Fourth grade students creating game "Tough Little Cookie" based on the story, "The Gingerbread Man."

Creating the Game Board

The *Stories on Board!* game board is a simple layout with the game based on chance, rather than skill. It is a racing game, where the objective is to move the game piece from a starting point to a finishing point on the board. Sequencing skills are strengthened as well as the ability to analyze and understand a story's structure. Students will also gain strategy skills as they map out their game boards.

Game Pieces

Nearly any small object may be used as a game piece or token. Here are some ideas:

- Coins
- Beans
- Buttons
- Large rhinestones
- Small pom-poms

Types of Game Boards

- The Square—like the board game Monopoly®, the game board is designed in a square shape. Game pieces begin and end on the same corner.
- The Spiral—the spiral game board moves game pieces from the outside to the inside in a spiral pattern.
- The Winding Path—the winding path is a random pattern that twists and turns. Game pieces start at one end and finish at an opposite end.
- The Rectangle—the rectangle board uses a zig-zagging or back-and-forth movement like Chutes and Ladders® to propel the game pieces forward.

Creating the Game Board

First, have students label the back of each game board with their names, teacher's name, and grade. If students are working in a group, the board should be labeled with the name of each group member. Students should give the game a creative title. For instance, a game based on the story "Jack and the Beanstalk" could be called "Racing Up the Beanstalk." Once the game boards are completed, they can be laminated for durability.

The layout of the game must be mapped using poster board. A successful *Stories on Board!* game has at least 25 to 30 spaces. The more spaces the game contains, the more opportunities the game creator(s) has(ve) to place perils, aids, and triumphs. In addition, the game becomes more fun and challenging. Each game board should have at least three perils and three triumphs to be a successful game. The game should accommodate between two and six players.

Students must problem-solve using basic math when creating their board game spaces. For instance, if a space says, "Go back 6 spaces," the space the player lands on must be blank and not contain a triumph (go forward ___ spaces).

Common Game Elements

The following are elements that can be included in the game to create tension and a challenging playing atmosphere:

- Game Board Perils
  - Lose a turn
  - Skip a turn
  - Go back to start
  - Go back ___ spaces
  - Wrong turn (move back)
  - Roll a ___ to escape

- Game Board Aids
  - Detour (move forward)
  - Shortcut (move forward)
- Game Board Triumph
  - Move ahead ___ spaces
  - Switch with player in first place
  - Move a player to anywhere on the board
  - Roll (or spin) again to move forward

Game board perils should be matched with story perils, and game board triumphs should be matched with story triumphs. For example, on a Cinderella game board, a story peril is matched with a game board peril ("You lost your glass slipper. Go back 6 spaces. Oh no!). Story perils and triumphs can also be created in keeping with the theme of the story. For example, on a Rapunzel game board, a story triumph is matched with a game board triumph ("Rapunzel blows you a kiss. Move ahead 5 spaces.").

Have the students examine the characteristics of the characters. These qualities can be used to create perils and triumphs. Wicked witches and fairies are magical and can cast spells. On a Rapunzel game board, as players climb up the tower, the witch casts spells that become perils ("Poof. The witch turns you into a frog for 1 turn. Ribbit!").

Students should also have a clear game goal. The goal of the players in "Cinderella's Ball" is to get from the start (home) to the finish (the ball). The goal of the players

Students play "The GMan Chase" based on the story, "The Gingerbread Man."

in "Rapunzel's Tower" is to get from the start (bottom of the tower) to the finish (top of the tower to rescue Rapunzel).

Playing the Game

To play the game, students will need one die or a spinner and game pieces. When the die is rolled or the spinner is spun, the player moves her game piece ahead the number of spaces indicated on the die/spinner (If a student rolls a 3, she moves forward 3 spaces). If a player lands on a peril, an aid, or a triumph, she should follow the directions given on that space. The first player to reach the end, wins.

When using a die, place it in a small plastic Dixie cup. Have the student shake the cup and turn it upside down. This captures the die and prevents it from flying or bouncing across the surface. The student lifts the cup and the number displayed on the top of the die is the number she moves forward on the game board.

To start the game, the student who rolls/spins the highest number goes first. In the case of a tie, the die is rolled again. From that point, the players take turns, going clockwise (right to left). If students do not understand "clockwise," explain that clockwise is "moving from right to left in the direction of a clock's hands."

Students playing "Mouseopoly" based on the story, "The Lion and the Mouse."

Storing the Game

If the games are made on large poster board, the board can be folded in half and placed in large envelopes or a shirt box. You can also store game boards in a large clear plastic container, which will allow the boards to remain unfolded. An 8-½ × 11" game can be laminated and stored in an envelope. Place game pieces, spinners and dice in labeled zippered plastic bags.

Culminating Event: Game Day

Now it's time for fun! On Game Day, students play each others' games. If students worked individually on their game projects, they trade with each other. If groups of students worked together on the board game, groups can trade games. You could even coordinate a grade-wide game day where classes trade games with other classes.

If you are interested in students assessing each other's work, you can use the following assessment criteria:

• What was the title of the game?

• Did you understand the game?

• Were there three perils on the game board? Name a peril.

Third grade students play each others' games during a grade wide "Game Day."

- Were there three triumphs on the game board? Name a triumph.
- What was the goal of the game?
- Who were the characters of the game?
- Did you have fun playing the game?

Suggested Assessment Criteria for Game Boards

- Fulfill the task.
- Have a clear beginning/middle/end.
- Have at least three perils and triumphs.
- Cooperate and interact with the members of the group.

Groups assess themselves in terms of the preceding criteria. Discuss what they feel they did well, what they might change, what they could add or develop.

Stories on Board! Assessment Rubric

3 Mastery	2 Competence	1 Needs practice
• Created an elaborate game board with many drawings in full color. Game has starting and finishing points with a fully developed layout.	• Created a complex game board with a several drawings and starting and finishing points	• Created a basic game board with a few drawings and starting and finishing points
• Game contains three or more perils.	• Game contains at least two perils.	• Game contains at least one peril.
• Game contains three or more perils.	• Game contains at least two triumphs.	• Game contains at least one triumph.
• Game defines protagonist, antagonist, supporting characters, and aids.	• Game defines protagonist, antagonist, and aids.	• Game defines protagonist and antagonist.
• Game contains game pieces, number of players, and rules.	• Game contains game pieces and number of players.	• Game contains game pieces.

Lesson Extensions and Other Connections

- Have the students write a paragraph in which they discuss their feelings about the activity.

- What part of the lesson did they most enjoy?

- Did they enjoy working individually, with partners, or as a group?

- How did the individual students come together to create a group board game?

Research other folktales and have the class map the story to create a class board game to donate to the school library. Assign parts: researcher, story writers, and editors. Critique and evaluate the finished story as a group.

Reproducible Board Games for Grades K-2

The Gingerbread Jam

Start

Finish

Back to Start!

-1

-1

-2

+1

-2

+2

-4

Pig poly

The Little Red Hen's
Pizza Party

Game Board Patterns

Spiral

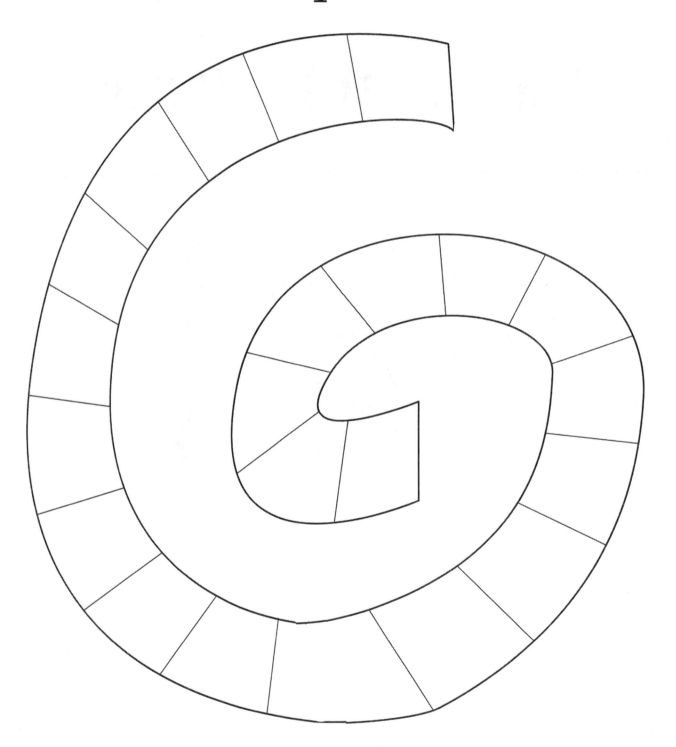

Square

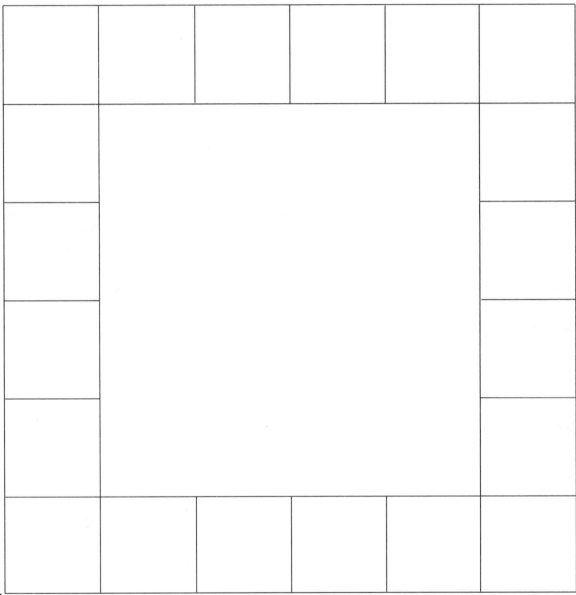

Start
Finish

Winding Path

Zig Zag

21	22	23	24
20	19	18	17
13	14	15	16
12	11	10	9
5	6	7	8
4	3	2	1

Stories

Anansi's Hat Shaking Dance

West Africa

At the beginning of time, spiders had long hair. But that was a very long time ago . . .

Anansi and his wife were getting ready for a party! It was Grandma's birthday. Anansi's wife was cooking up a big, delicious pot of beans for the party. She tasted the beans and said, "These beans are good but they need a little pepper. Let me look in the cupboard for some pepper."

So she opened the cupboard and looked. "Parsley, sage, rosemary, thyme . . . no pepper! I have to run out to get some more pepper." She called for her husband, "Anansi!"

He answered, "Yes, dear?!"

Anansi's wife said, "I have to get some more pepper. Will you watch the pot of beans for me?"

Anansi slurped his lips and said, "Yes, dear!"

Anansi's wife knew exactly what he was thinking and said, "Now, Anansi, whatever you do, you mustn't touch the beans. Do you understand?"

"Yes, dear."

His wife left and Anansi began decorating for the party. First, he blew up those big, colorful round things—what do you call them? Oh yes, balloons! Help me blow up the balloons! Then he began hanging up those long colorful paper things—what do you call them? Oh yes, streamers! Help me snip the streamers. When he was finished with that, he began setting the table—first the plates, then the glasses, then the silverware, and finally some napkins folded nicely on top of the plates. All that hard work was making Anansi very hungry! About that time, the aroma of the delicious beans floated in from the kitchen and the beans started to smell REALLY good.

27

From *Stories on Board! Creating Board Games from Favorite Tales* by Dianne de Las Casas. Illustrated by Soleil Lisette. Santa Barbara, CA: Libraries Unlimited. Copyright © 2010.

Anansi went into the kitchen. He looked into the pot of beans. His wife did ask him to "watch" the beans, didn't she? They sure LOOKED good. He took a big whiff of the beans. They sure SMELLED good.

So he stirred the beans.

He smelled the beans.

He tasted the beans.

Mmm. Mmm. Mmm.

They tasted good!

But one taste wasn't enough. Anansi said, "I'll just have a little more."

So he stirred the beans.

He smelled the beans.

He tasted the beans.

Mmm. Mmm. Mmm.

They tasted good!

By now, you can imagine tasting the beans was too much for Anansi. He wanted more!

So he stirred the beans.

He smelled the beans.

He tasted the beans.

Mmm. Mmm. Mmm.

They tasted good!

Before Anansi knew it, he had eaten more than half the beans in the pot! "One more small itsy bitsy, teensy weensy, tiny winy little taste couldn't hurt," thought Anansi. He was getting ready to put some more beans in his mouth when he heard the door.

"Anansi, it's me and Grandma's with me!" his wife called out.

He heard them walking into the kitchen. He had to think of something and fast! He had to hide the beans! Quickly, he grabbed Grandma's party hat, dumped the beans into the hat, and placed the hat on his head, just as his wife and Grandma were walking into the kitchen.

Now if you know anything about beans coming out of a pot, you know that they are hot! They were so hot they were burning the top of Anansi's head! He couldn't stand still and he began shaking and moving around.

His wife asked, "Anansi! What are you doing?"

Anansi answered, "Uh, uh, I am doing a new dance for Grandma's party. Yeah, that's it. It's called Anansi's Hat Shaking Dance!"

Grandma said, "Oooh! It looks like fun! I want to dance." And she began to shake and move around, just like Anansi.

Anansi's wife looked at Grandma and Anansi shaking and moving and groovin', so she too began to dance!

But all that movin' and shakin' was a movin' and a shakin' those beans. The heat on top of Anansi's head was too much! The beans began to drip down the side of his face—down his cheeks, down his neck, and even in his ears! Eeeeww! Finally, he couldn't take it anymore and he jerked off the hat.

Anansi's wife cried out, "Anansi, just what did you think you were doing." She put her hands on her hips, just like your mama does when she's mad.

Anansi smiled sheepishly at his wife and said, "I couldn't help it!"

I stirred the beans.

I smelled the beans.

I tasted the beans.

Mmm. Mmm. Mmm.

They tasted good!

Anansi's wife looked into the pot and saw how much of the beans were missing. "Anansi!" she cried out.

But Grandma started laughing hysterically. She pointed to Anansi's head and said, "Boy, you are as bald as a bowling ball!" Anansi's wife started laughing too and Grandma said she never laughed so hard in all her life. It was one of the funniest, best birthday gifts she had ever received. And because Grandma was happy, everyone was happy.

There was still a little bit of beans left in the pot so they shared.

They stirred the beans.

They smelled the beans.

They tasted the beans.

Mmm. Mmm. Mmm.

They tasted good!

They had a great time at Grandma's birthday party and even danced a brand new dance—Anansi's Hat Shaking Dance. To this day, if you look at a spider, you will see that he is still bald and he sure knows how to dance!

The Ant and the Grasshopper

Aesop Fable from Greece

It was springtime and Grasshopper was busy singing a song. Soon, Ant came by dragging some food behind him. Ant was:

Pushing and pulling and tugging and lugging.

Grasshopper said, "Why don't you stop working and play with me?"

Ant answered, "I am too busy preparing for the winter."

"Suit yourself," sang Grasshopper.

Spring turned into summer and Grasshopper was busy singing a song. Ant came by dragging some food behind him. Ant was:

Pushing and pulling and tugging and lugging.

Grasshopper said, "Why don't you stop working and play with me?"

Ant answered, "I am too busy preparing for the winter."

"Suit yourself," sang Grasshopper.

Well, summer turned into fall and Grasshopper was busy singing a song. Ant came by dragging some food behind him. Ant was:

Pushing and pulling and tugging and lugging.

Grasshopper said, "Why don't you stop working and play with me?"

Ant answered, "I am too busy preparing for the winter."

"Suit yourself," sang Grasshopper.

Fall turned into winter. Because Grasshopper sang all year long, he didn't gather any food. He lay in the snow cold and hungry. When Ant came by and saw Grasshopper, he took pity. Ant said, "I'll take you in tonight, Grasshopper, but you must sing for your supper!"

If you don't work hard, you could find yourself out in the cold!

Beauty and the Beast

France

There was once a merchant who had six sons and six daughters. The merchant did very well and provided for his children nicely until one day, something tragic happened. Their beautiful house, with all of its furnishings, burned to the ground. More misfortune came to them when the merchant learned that all of his ships had either been lost to sea, ravaged by pirates, or burned by fire. They were forced to live a life of simplicity, a life to which no one was accustomed. But the youngest daughter, Beauty, who was both pretty and clever, did all she could to make the best of things while her brothers and sisters mumbled and grumbled and continually complained.

One day, the merchant found out that one of his ships had been recovered. This was good news, for now they would once again have the things they had been living without. The merchant made preparations to set out for the ship. Beauty's brothers and sisters asked the merchant for all sorts of finery. It was Beauty who remained silent. The merchant noticed that his youngest daughter was quiet and he asked, "And what shall I bring back for you, Beauty?"

She answered, "All I wish is for your safe return home, Father."

This answer puzzled her brothers and sisters as well as her father. "Surely there must be something I can bring back to you, Beauty," the merchant said.

"Well, dear father, if you insist, I beg that you bring me back a single rose. I have not seen one in so long and I do love them so much."

So the merchant set off and reached town quickly. When he arrived, he found that the goods from his ship had been divided amongst his former business companions and there was barely enough left over to cover the cost of the journey home. To make matters worse, he was forced to travel home in snowy weather. Cold, tired, and

33

hungry, he traveled through rough terrain and dense forest. His horse was weary and the merchant knew that it could not go on much longer. He needed to find shelter and quickly.

Presently, he came to a clearing in the forest and saw, in the distance, a splendid castle. The grounds were barely covered with snow and he could see orange trees laden with fruit and flowers of all colors. He approached the castle and dismounted the horse. The door was ajar so he went inside. It was warm and he could smell the pleasant aroma of hot food. He searched the castle for any inhabitants but found only silence in answer to his calls. He found a room where a clear fire was burning in the fireplace and a couch was drawn near the fire. Thinking he would wait for the host of the house, he sat on the couch and fell asleep.

In the morning, he awoke to find a tray of food prepared for him, ready and waiting. Though he again searched, he found no servants and no sign of life anywhere! He began to wander around the enchanting castle and found himself walking through the garden outside. The sun was shining and birds were happily flying about, chirping in musical harmony. The flowers bloomed, and the air was soft and sweet. He was marveling at the beauty of the garden when he spotted the most beautiful rose bush he had ever seen. The roses were an exquisite color of deep red, with petals as soft as silk. They reminded him of his promise to Beauty, and he reached down to pluck a tender rose from the bush.

Suddenly, he heard a strange, loud noise behind him. He turned around to find the most hideous beast staring angrily at him. The beast bellowed, "Who gave you permission to gather my roses? Wasn't it enough that I allowed you into my home, gave you a warm place to sleep, and fed you and your horse?! Is this the way you show your gratitude by stealing my roses?! You will not go unpunished!"

The beast towered over the merchant as he looked up, his eyes filled with fear. The merchant dropped the fatal rose and cried, "Pardon me, noble sir. I am truly grateful for your kind hospitality and I meant you no harm. I did not imagine that you would be offended by my taking a single rose."

The merchant's speech did nothing to lessen the beast's anger. The merchant cried out, "If only my daughter, Beauty, could know what danger her rose has brought me to." The beast then commanded the merchant to tell him about Beauty and the merchant did so.

After the merchant finished his story, the beast said, in a less furious tone, "I will forgive you if you give me one of your daughters."

The merchant cried out, "I cannot do that, sir. How can I possibly ask one of my daughters to trade her life for mine? And what excuse could I use to lure her here?"

The beast answered, "No excuse will be necessary. If she comes, she must come of her own will. If any of your daughters is courageous enough and loves you enough, she will come. I will give you one month to fulfill my wish. If after one month, you do not return with one of your daughters, you will meet your doom."

The merchant had no choice. He could not defy the beast. He went back to his room and prepared for his journey home the next day. In the morning, the beast came to visit. "Did you sleep well?" he asked the merchant.

The merchant answered hesitantly, "Yes. Thank you."

The beast motioned to the front of the castle. The horse you will ride is ready and waiting for you. You will go home and, in one month, return here. The horse knows the way and will bring you back. Farewell and remember your promise. And here, bring this to Beauty," the beast handed the merchant a single red rose.

The merchant sped away on the horse the beast gave him and soon found himself at home once again. The brothers and sisters were excited to see their father return home and began burdening him with questions. Everyone but Beauty asked, "What did you bring back home, father?"

Sadly the merchant sighed. "Only this," he held up the rose and looked at Beauty. Her face lit up as she beheld the exquisite rose. The merchant said, "It does not come without a price," and he went on to tell the story of the beast.

The brothers and sisters were angry with Beauty, for her simple request cost their father so much. If she had not asked for the rose, he may have come home with treasures for all of them. And now, one of the daughters had to live with the Beast in his castle.

Beauty looked at her father and said, "Oh father, had I only known! I would never have asked for such a simple thing. Since I caused such misfortune, I should go. I will live with the beast and keep your promise to him."

At first, the merchant would not allow it, saying that he could not ask Beauty to trade her life for his. But Beauty was insistent and, in the end, won out. Near the end of the month, Beauty packed her things and bid goodbye to her brothers and sisters.

Beauty and the merchant set off for the castle on the same horse the merchant rode home. The horse knew the way and soon they arrived at the castle. Beauty marveled at the splendid sights of the castle. When they went inside, the table was set with a hot meal prepared for them. They had hardly finished their meal when the beast's footsteps could be heard. Beauty clung to her father in fear. When the beast appeared, Beauty did her best to mask her fear and greeted him respectfully. This seemed to please the beast.

The beast ordered Beauty and her father to their rooms, instructing Beauty to help her father load two traveling trunks with treasures from the castle. Beauty and her father did as they were told and loaded the trunks with gowns for her sisters, gold, delicate china, jewels, and warm coats for her brothers. The chests seemed to never fill up but finally, they were ready.

The next morning, Beauty and her father found the trunks already loaded onto a horse-drawn carriage. Beauty kissed her father goodbye and felt sure she would never see him again. The merchant knew that he must leave at once in order that he not anger the beast. Quickly, he departed.

The next morning, Beauty was alone and sad. After some time, she adjusted to living at the castle. During the day, she wandered through the castle looking for things to amuse herself. She found fascinating books in the library, a magical theater in which she could see plays and dances, and of course, the lovely garden. She always admired the roses but never dared to touch them. In the evenings, she would sit down for dinner and the beast would join her. At first, she was merely polite, fearing him. But gradually, she came to like him and enjoyed the time they spent together. Some evenings, they would even dance to music Beauty loved.

Then the beast began asking her, "Beauty, will you marry me?" And although she cared for him, she always said no. Every night when she slept, she would dream of a handsome prince who always warned her not to be deceived by appearances. She grew to love the prince of her dreams and wished that he was real.

Though the beast was kind and good to her, Beauty longed to see her family again. She began to grow restless. She ate less and did not talk much. "Beauty, what is wrong?" Beast asked.

"I want to see my family again," she answered.

"Is it that you are so repulsed by me that you do not want to be around me and wish to return home?" the beast asked in agony.

"No, dear Beast, I just miss my father, and my brothers and sisters. I wish only to visit. I promise I would return here and live the rest of my life with you."

"I will grant your wish, Beauty. Fill four boxes with gifts for your brothers and sisters and take this ring. When you wish to return to me, you need only to place it on your finger and say, 'I wish to see my Beast again.' After you go to sleep tonight, in the morning you will find yourself at home. Remember to return back to me within two months or I will surely die."

"I will return, my dear Beast, I promise." Beauty said.

Beauty filled four boxes with gifts for her brothers and sisters then went to sleep. In the morning, she found herself at home again. He father, brothers, and sisters rejoiced to see her home. She told them how kind the beast was and gave them their gifts. She was happy at home for a while, but she noticed that she did not dream of her precious prince and she began to miss the kind warmth of the beast.

One night, a day after she was to return to the beast, she had a terrible dream. She dreamed that she was walking through the garden when she heard the groans of the beast. When she found him, he was dying. Beauty was so distressed by this dream that she announced her intention of returning to the castle at once. She placed the ring on her finger and said, "I wish to see my Beast again."

When Beauty opened her eyes, she found herself back at the castle. She began searching the castle for the beast but could not find him. She ran up and down the avenues of the garden, desperately calling out his name, "Beast! Beast!" She heard no answer. Finally, she saw the same place in her dreams. There she found the beast, lying on the ground.

She stroked his head and cried, "Beast, Beast wake up." But he did not open his eyes.

"Please don't leave me!" Beauty cried. She bent down and kissed his forehead gently and suddenly, his eyes fluttered open.

"Oh Beast, you gave me such a terrible fright! I thought you were gone forever. I didn't realize how much I love you until I thought you were gone!" Beauty threw her arms around the beast.

Beast spoke faintly, "Can you really love someone such as me?"

"Of course," she answered softly as she held his hand.

Then he lifted up his head and whispered, "Will you marry me, Beauty?"

Beauty answered, "Yes, dear Beast."

As she spoke, a blaze of light surrounded them and the words "Long Live the Prince and His Bride" were formed by the dancing light of fireflies.

Beauty turned to ask the beast what it meant. As she gazed up, she saw a prince standing before her with his hand held out to help her up. It was the prince of her dreams. "Who are you?" she asked.

"I am the beast and the prince of your dreams. I am the one you love, Beauty, and the one who loves you."

Overjoyed, Beauty leaped into his arms. He said, "Come with me, I have a gift for you, Beauty."

He led her to the avenue of roses and plucked a tender red rose from its bush. He handed it to her. Beauty looked up as the prince bent down and kissed her tenderly.

At the wedding feast, her brothers, sisters, and father were all there, rejoicing in the good fortune. And they danced joyously the rest of the night to Beauty's favorite music.

And they lived . . . happily ever after.

Brer Rabbit and the Tar Baby

Southern United States

Brer Rabbit was a rascally rabbit. He was always tricking folks and getting the best of them. Brer Fox was tired of it and decided he was going to get back at Brer Rabbit. So Brer Fox mixed tar with turpentine and made a sticky, gooey concoction. He shaped it into a person and stuck a straw hat on top. He called it the "Tar Baby."

It was a hot day and Brer Fox set the tar baby in the middle of the road on the way to the well. He knew that Brer Rabbit would come by soon. He hid low behind the bushes waiting for Brer Rabbit. Sure enough, Brer Rabbit came hopping down the road.

Lippity-clippity. Clippity-lippity.

Brer Fox said, "That Brer Rabbit sure is as sassy as a jaybird" and he stayed hidden low in the bushes, watching. Brer Rabbit saw the tar baby in the middle of the road and stopped to say hello.

Hello, ma'am, how're you doing today?

Nice weather we're having, wouldn't you say?

But the tar baby didn't say a word. She just stared at Brer Rabbit. Brer Rabbit said, "Didn't you hear a word I just said? I said . . .

Hello, ma'am, how're you doing today?

Nice weather we're having, wouldn't you say?

But the tar baby still didn't say a word. Brer Rabbit was angry. "If you don't take off that hat and say hello good and proper, I'm going to teach you a lesson!" Still, the tar baby didn't say a word. So Brer Rabbit pulled back his right fist and swung.

SMACK! Brer Rabbit's right fist got stuck.

Brer Fox watched from the bushes where he was hidden and began to laugh. Brer Rabbit was even angrier. "If you don't let me loose, I'm going to knock you silly!" Still, the tar baby didn't say a word. So Brer Rabbit pulled back his left fist and swung.

SMACK! Brer Rabbit's left fist got stuck.

Brer Fox kept on watching from the bushes where he was hidden and laughed at Brer Rabbit. By now, Brer Rabbit was furious. "Let me loose before I kick the stuffing out of you!" he yelled at the tar baby. Still, the tar baby didn't say a word. So Brer Rabbit pulled back his right foot and kicked.

SMACK! Brer Rabbit's right foot got stuck!

By this time, Brer Rabbit was good and stuck. His fur was covered with ooey, gooey, icky, sticky black tar. Brer Fox couldn't take it anymore! He sprung out from behind the bushes and laughed. "Brer Rabbit, you look sort of stuck this morning! You've been acting like the boss of the plantation, tricking folks and getting the best of them. Now I got you good!"

Brer Rabbit couldn't loose himself because he was good and stuck. Brer Fox said, "Funny thing is—you got yourself into that mess trying to teach a lesson. Let's see you get yourself out of this mess! Stay here while I get some brush pile so I can start a fire. I'm having barbecue today!"

Brer Rabbit said, "You can roast me but whatever you do . . .

DON'T THROW ME IN THE BRIAR PATCH.

Brer Fox couldn't find any brush pile so he said, "Maybe I'll boil you. It'll be easier." Brer Rabbit said, "You can boil me but whatever you do . . .

DON'T THROW ME IN THE BRIAR PATCH.

Brer Fox couldn't find any water so he said, "Maybe I'll tie you up and save you for later." Brer Rabbit said, "You can tie me up but whatever you do . . .

DON'T THROW ME IN THE BRIAR PATCH.

Brer Fox couldn't find any rope so he said, "I'm going to throw you into the briar patch!" He pulled Brer Rabbit from the tar baby and flung him by his back legs into the briar patch.

Brer Rabbit flew into the briar patch, right into the bushes. A minute later, Brer Rabbit stuck his head out and yelled at Brer Fox. "It's too bad you lost your catch! I was born and bred in the briar patch!" He stuck out his tongue at Brer Fox and hopped away.

Lippity-clippity. Clippity-lippity.

Brer Rabbit was a rascally rabbit. He was always tricking folks and getting the best of them. The end.

Briar Rose (Sleeping Beauty)

Germany

In olden times, there lived a King and a Queen. More than anything, they wanted a child but years passed and their wish lay idle. One day, as the Queen was bathing and dreaming of her wish once again, a frog skipped out of the water and said to her, "Your wish shall be fulfilled. Before a year passes, to you a daughter shall be born."

As the frog uttered it, so it came to pass. A little girl was born who was so beautiful that all who came to gaze upon her fell in love. Her name was Rose. To celebrate their good fortune, the King ordered a great feast. To this great fête, he invited family, friends, and the wise women of the kingdom, who were fairies. There were 13 wise women in his dominion but because he only had 12 golden plates, he left one uninvited.

On the day of the great feast, the 12 fairies presented their gifts upon the baby. One wise woman blessed her with virtue, another with beauty, another with riches, and so on. Just as the eleventh fairy had bestowed her gift, suddenly a great wind shook the banquet hall. The 13th wise woman was in a fury because she had not been invited. She gazed upon the innocent infant and hissed, "When the Princess turns fifteen, she shall prick herself with a spindle and die!" With a flourish, she turned her back upon the King, the Queen, and all the guests, and disappeared.

The 12th fairy had not yet bestowed her gift. She said, "I cannot undo what has been gifted but I can perhaps soften it. On her fifteenth birthday, when Princess Rose pricks her finger on the spindle, she shall not die. Instead, she shall fall into a sleep of one hundred years."

The King, who was outraged at the evil gift, wished to protect his darling daughter so he ordered that every spindle in the kingdom be burned. But fate has a way of intervening. On Rose's 15th birthday, she wandered through the castle and began climbing

41

the stairs of an old tower. At the top of the tower was a small room. In the door's lock was a rusty key. Curiosity burned. Rose wanted to see what was behind the door. She turned the key and was surprised to find an old woman with a spindle, spinning flax.

Princess Rose curtsied and said, "Good day, my lady. What are you doing here?"

"I am spinning," answered the old woman.

Rose had never seen such an invention. Being a girl of adventurous spirit, she longed to try something new. "Today I am fifteen years old. I should like to try my hand at spinning."

The old woman clucked. "Spinning is a skill, an art. Only the pure of heart can weave a thread so fine."

Rose smiled, "May I please try, my lady? You can teach me."

The old woman grinned. "Very well. What the Princess wants, the Princess gets."

Princess Rose had scarcely sat down when she pricked her finger on the spindle. As a single drop of blood fell to the floor, the prophecy came to pass. Rose fell into a nearby bed and closed her eyes, falling into a dreamless sleep. In that same moment, a hush fell over the kingdom. The breeze stopped blowing. The birds ceased chirping. Time itself came to a halt as the entire kingdom fell asleep to a hundred-year lullaby.

Around the castle, a hedge of briars grew. The briars grew as heavy as the legend that surrounded the land. Tales of the beautiful Briar Rose enchanted generations of young men, who tried to fight their way through the stinging nettles only to find themselves woefully defeated. Many of these daring youth lost their lives in the tangle of thorns that covered the castle.

One day, after 99 years and 364 days had passed, a young prince from another country strode into town on a magnificent white stallion. He asked the townsfolk if the legend was true.

"Don't be foolish, lad," scolded a leathery old man pointing with one hand and holding a pair of fish in the other. "Many have lost their lives to the fancy of that poisonous story."

But the young prince was not thwarted. The legendary tales of Briar Rose and her inimitable beauty had traveled worldwide. "I have not come all this way to fail," declared the mighty prince.

The old man waved him off, shaking his head. "A greater fool I have never seen."

After eating a hot meal and feeding carrots to his horse, the young prince rode to the castle of Briar Rose. It was as all the stories had proclaimed, as though time's very breath had frozen in midair. Though a full, fluorescent moon shone above, the briars were so dense, the prince could not see the castle. The thorns served as an impenetrable wall protecting its golden treasure inside.

But suddenly, at the stroke of midnight, a strange thing happened. When the prince touched the briars with his silver sword, they shrunk back and cherry roses began blooming. A path opened and he rode to the castle, where the miracle continued. Doves spread their wings, cats stretched, and dogs slowly wagged their tales. Pots banged, children shouted, and spouses argued. It was the cacophony of life reborn.

The prince dismounted his steed and hurried to the tower where he knew the princess lay. Bounding the winding stairs, he arrived to find the door locked. He glanced down and saw a rusty key on the floor. He inserted the key into the lock and turned.

Lying on a bed was the most exquisite woman he had ever had the fortune to lay his eyes upon. Her very countenance took away his breath. He knelt down and took her hand. "Briar Rose, it is time to rise."

Princess Rose's eyes fluttered open. She felt joy radiating from the handsome stranger kneeling before her. By and by, the wedding of the Prince and Briar Rose was celebrated with great splendor. To the end of their lives, they lived happy and contented.

Cinderella

France

Once upon a time, in a kingdom far away, there lived a pretty young girl named Ella. Her mother died and her father remarried a wicked woman with two equally wicked daughters. Ella's father was often away so she was alone with her stepmother and two stepsisters, Bertha and Agatha. They made Ella do all the work from sunup until sundown. She even had to clean the soot and cinders from the fireplace. They began calling her "Cinderella."

Bertha yelled, "Cinderella, draw my bath."

Agatha screamed, "Cinderella, turn down my bed."

Of course, kind and goodhearted Cinderella did everything she was told. Her stepsisters made fun of her and flaunted their beautiful clothes in front of her while Cinderella wore rags covered in grime and soot.

It was a beautiful day when the good news arrived. A royal messenger from the king's castle announced, "The prince is seeking a bride. Every maiden in the kingdom must attend the Prince's Royal Ball at the castle on Saturday night at 7:00 o'clock. It is an order!"

Cinderella's heart leapt for joy. *Every maiden* she thought to herself. *That means me too!* She planned to sew the most exquisite gown. It was then her stepmother spoke, "Cinderella, you cannot attend the ball. There is simply too much work for you to do here. You'll have to stay home."

Cinderella was crushed but she said nothing and did as she was told. Hours before the ball, Bertha and Agatha shouted orders to Cinderella. "Press my dress! Shine my shoes. Polish my pearls!" Cinderella tried to do everything at once.

45

Finally, Cinderella's stepmother and her two stepsisters were ready. They disdainfully dismissed Cinderella and boarded their carriage. Off they raced to the Prince's Royal Ball.

Cinderella rushed inside and finished her chores. She had just enough time to get ready. She pulled a dress out of the closet and tried it on, but it was too small. She could not go to the ball after all. Cinderella collapsed and cried.

"Cinderella, dry your tears," a voice said gently.

Cinderella looked up and saw a small woman with shimmering wings. "I am your fairy godmother."

"What do you mean?" asked Cinderella.

"This is what I mean." The fairy godmother swished her wand and Cinderella was bedecked in a bedazzling ball gown. Then the fairy godmother looked down at Cinderella's bare feet. "Oh that will never do!" A swirl of the wand and Cinderella's feet sparkled in glass slippers.

Cinderella stood astonished. "Hurry up now," said the fairy godmother, "there's no time to waste. At the stroke of midnight, you must take flight or all will be as it was before. You'll be a servant girl and nothing more."

"Thank you!" exclaimed Cinderella. She boarded a carriage and was swiftly whisked away to the ball. Upon entry into the castle, everyone stopped in their tracks. Cinderella was a stunning presence. Immediately, the prince took notice. He walked her way and asked for a dance.

"Who is she?" was the question of the night. The prince would not leave Cinderella's side for even a moment. No one else could get a dance with the prince. The stepsisters fumed with fury.

Cinderella and the prince danced all night long. But as suddenly as the night began, it ended. The clock struck midnight. "BONG. BONG. BONG."

Cinderella panicked. "Oh, I have to go." She ran from the prince, dashing down the castle stairs.

The prince cried, "Wait!" but it was too late. The fair maiden was gone. She did, however, leave a clue behind—her sparkling slipper slipped off and sat on the stairs.

The prince picked it up and proclaimed, "Only the maiden whose foot fits this slipper will be my bride." He began a kingdom-wide search.

Every maiden short and tall, big and small, tried in vain to fit the slipper but it was a hard shoe to fill. The prince had big expectations but everyone fell short. He finally arrived at Cinderella's house. Bertha and Agatha batted their eyelashes and smiled sweetly at the prince but their charms fell flat. Neither one of them could fit the shoe.

"Is there no other maiden in this house?" asked the prince.

"I haven't tried it on," said Cinderella as she stepped out of the shadows.

Cinderella's stepmother spoke. "She is nothing but a maid servant. She didn't even attend the ball. She's not worth your time."

The prince emphasized, "*Every* maiden tries on the slipper. Please come this way." He beckoned Cinderella.

She sat down in front of the prince and put her foot forward. Much to his delight, the slipper slid easily on Cinderella's foot. She reached into her pocket and pulled out the other sparkling slipper.

"No! No! No! No! No!" screamed the wicked stepsisters. They both threw a terrible temper tantrum.

The prince smiled at Cinderella. "I knew I would find you. You're the only maiden who could fill a princess's shoes."

Cinderella and the prince were, of course, married and they lived happily ever after.

The Frog Prince

Germany

In the olden time, when wishing was having, there lived a king who had beautiful daughters. But the youngest daughter was exceedingly beautiful. She wore crisp dresses that were pressed just so, and she always made sure that her hair received 100 brush strokes every morning and every night. To her father, she was Priscilla. But to everyone else, she was Princess Prissy. Even the Sun himself was enchanted by her every time she came out into the sunshine.

Near the castle was a great forest. In the midst of this forest stood a large tree, whose branches hung over a peaceful pond. Whenever it was very hot, the princess would run off into the forest and sit down by the pond. When she became bored, she would toss a golden ball up into the air and catch it. Up and down. Up and down. Up and down. She spent many hours amusing herself this way. The golden ball was by far her favorite toy and she loved playing with it.

One day the princess went into the forest and sat by the pond, tossing her ball as usual. Up and down. Up and down. Up and down. It just so happened that she tossed the ball into the air and the ball fell onto the grass and rolled past her into the pond. She could do nothing to stop it. Kerplash! The water in the pond was so deep that she could not see into it, and she realized that her ball had disappeared. The princess was so distraught that she began to lament and wail, crying her eyes out.

"My ball, my golden ball! It's gone!"

As she cried, a voice called out, "Why do you cry, O King's daughter? Your tears would move even the trees to weep." She turned around and saw a big, green frog stretching his thick, head out of the water.

49

"Oh you old frog. Was it you that spoke? I am crying for my golden ball for it has slipped away and rolled into the water."

The frog answered, "Please do not cry princess. I can help you but what would you give me if I fetched your golden ball?"

"What could you want, old frog?" asked the princess. "I could offer you my pretty, starched dresses, pearls, and jewels, or my golden crown."

The frog replied, "I have no use for dresses, jewels, or golden crowns. I wish only that you love me, be my friend, allow me to sit at your table, eat from your golden plate, drink from your silver cup, dance with me after dinner, and sleep in your feather soft bed. If you promise me all this, I will dive down and fetch your golden ball."

"Oh, I will promise you all, if only you will fetch my ball," said Princess Prissy slyly. But she secretly thought to herself, "What a silly frog. I cannot allow such a creature into the castle."

The frog, hearing her promise, dove swiftly into the water and retrieved the golden ball.

As soon as the frog handed the princess the golden ball, she squealed with delight and ran off without another word to the frog.

"Stop! Stop!" the frog cried out. "Take me with you. I cannot run as fast as you!"

But Prissy did not stop. She ran all the way home to the castle, forgetting the frog and her promise. The next day, the princess was sitting at the table with her father and all his courtiers.

She was eating from her golden plate when they all heard something coming up the stairs.

"Splishy, splashy, splashy, splish.
The princess is bound to keep her promise."

When it arrived at the top of the stairs, it knocked on the door and said,

"Splishy, splashy, splashy, splish.
The princess is bound to keep her promise."

The king urged his daughter to open the door and when she did, she saw the ugly frog and immediately slammed the door. She sat back down at the table looking very pale.

The king looked at his daughter alarmed and asked, "Priscilla, what is the matter? Is it a giant come to fetch you away?"

The princess looked down and answered, "Oh no, father, it is only an ugly frog."

The king asked, "What? A frog? What is a frog doing here?"

Princess Prissy answered, "Yesterday, when I was playing with my golden ball by the pond, my ball rolled into the pond. The frog fetched it for me because I promised him that he could be my friend. I never thought that he would come out of the water but now he's here!"

At that moment, there was another knock on the door, and a voice said,

"Splishy, splashy, splashy, splish.

The princess is bound to keep her promise."

The princess cried, "What shall I do, Father?"

The king answered, "What you have promised, you must keep. Open the door and let in the frog." So the princess did as she was told and reluctantly opened the door. The frog followed her to the table, hopped up onto the table, and sat next to the princess. He began to eat from her golden plate and drink from her silver cup. The princess watched in disgust. The frog offered her a drink and she shook her head no.

Then the frog hopped down and said,

"Princess, keep your promise, here's your chance.

Turn on the music and let us dance!"

The princess folded her arms across her chest and said, "As if!"

But her father looked at her sternly and said, "What you have promised, you must keep." The princess reluctantly picked up the frog and began to dance with him around the room.

After they finished dancing, the frog said, "All this dancing has made me tired. I am ready to sleep on your feather soft bed as you have promised."

The princess looked at her father and pleaded, "Father do I HAVE to?"

The king answered, "What you have promised, you must keep."

The princess placed the frog on the end of the bed. "There, you awful frog, stay down there! Sleep as you will. You cannot lie on my pillow. I am not lying next to a cold frog! You might mess up my hair!"

At this, the frog began to lament and wail. The princess cried out, "Frog, why do you cry so?"

The frog answered, "All my life, all I have wanted is a friend. I helped you, fetched your golden ball, and now you don't even want to be near me. You judge me by how I look on the outside and not what is on the inside."

The princess looked down thoughtfully, then sat on the bed next to the frog. The frog's words touched her heart. Softly, she said, "You are right, dear frog, you have been kind to me and I have shown you no hospitality or friendship. I am sorry." The princess bent down, picked up the frog, and hugged him.

As soon as she did, a magical transformation took place. The frog changed into a handsome prince. He smiled at her and said, "You have broken the evil witch's spell, princess. You gave friendship to an ugly creature. You looked beyond the exterior and saw the goodness inside. For that I thank you."

The princess was delighted. She hugged the Frog Prince and they danced joyfully around the room. From that time forward, the princess and the Frog Prince were friends and the princess always treated every creature with kindness.

The Gingerbread Man

England

There was once a hungry old woman who one day decided to make a gingerbread man. She put the ingredients into a big bowl and began stirring up the batter. Then she poured the batter onto a pan in the shape of a gingerbread man. She put him in the oven and waited for him to bake.

Tick tock, tick tock

Tick tock, tick tock, tick tock . . . DING!

The gingerbread man was ready and the old woman couldn't wait to see how he turned out. She opened up the oven and placed the pan on the counter. When the gingerbread man cooled down, she iced two eyes and a smiling mouth on his face, two strips on the end of each arm, two strips at the bottom of each leg, and finally, two buttons on his chest. When the old woman was finished, suddenly, the Gingerbread Man jumped up and yelled, "Hey!" And he began running away!

The old woman cried out, "Stop, Gingerbread Man, stop!" But the gingerbread man kept running with a jump, a skip and a hop. And as he ran, he said,

"Run, baby, run as fast as you can

You can't catch me 'cause I'm the (clap, clap) Gingerbread Man!"

The gingerbread man ran away from the old woman until he came upon a pen. In that pen was a (oink, oink) . . . pig! The pig eyed the gingerbread man hungrily and licked his lips. "Won't you stop Gingerbread Man and join me for . . . breakfast?"

But the gingerbread man would not stop. He jumped up and yelled, "Hey!" And he began running away!

The pig cried out, "Stop, Gingerbread Man, stop!" But the gingerbread man kept running with a jump, a skip and a hop. And as he ran, he said,

"Run, baby, run as fast as you can

You can't catch me 'cause I'm the (clap, clap) Gingerbread Man!"

The gingerbread man ran away from the old woman and the pig until he came upon a fence. Behind that fence was a (neigh, neigh) . . . horse! The horse eyed the gingerbread man hungrily and licked his lips. "Won't you stop Gingerbread Man and join me for . . . lunch?"

But the gingerbread man would not stop. He jumped up and yelled, "Hey!" And he began running away!

The horse cried out, "Stop, Gingerbread Man, stop!" But the gingerbread man kept running with a jump, a skip and a hop. And as he ran, he said,

"Run, baby, run as fast as you can

You can't catch me 'cause I'm the (clap, clap) Gingerbread Man!"

The gingerbread man ran away from the old woman, the pig, and the horse until he came upon a field. In that field was a (moo, moo) . . . cow! The cow eyed the gingerbread man hungrily and licked his lips. "Won't you stop Gingerbread Man and join me for . . . dinner?!"

But the gingerbread man would not stop. He jumped up and yelled, "Hey!" And he began running away!

The cow cried out, "Stop, Gingerbread Man, stop!" But the gingerbread man kept running with a jump, a skip and a hop. And as he ran, he said,

"Run, baby, run as fast as you can

You can't catch me 'cause I'm the (clap, clap) Gingerbread Man!"

The gingerbread man ran away from the old woman, the pig, the horse, and the cow until he came upon a cold, deep river. He wanted to cross the river but there was a problem. Gingerbread Man didn't know how to swim.

There, at the river's edge, was a feisty . . . fox! The fox said, "Gingerbread Man! Would you like to cross the river?"

Gingerbread Man said, "I don't know how to swim."

Fox answered, "No problem! Hop on my back and I will swim you across. When we get to the other side, you can join me for a . . . SNACK!" Gingerbread Man foolishly agreed and hopped on top of the fox's back.

The fox began swimming into the midst of the river and the water got deeper and deeper and deeper until Gingerbread Man had to climb right on top of fox's long snout. Then fox said, "From the top of my back to the tip of my nose, you'll be my snack. That's the way it goes!"

The fox jumped up and yelled, "Hey!" And he began gobbling away.

From the pan, he ran and ran but now that's the end of the Gingerbread Man. And that, my friends, is the end of that.

Goldie Locks and the Three Bears

England

Deep in the forest, there lived three bears. There was Papa Bear. There was Mama Bear. And there was Baby Bear.

BAM. BAM. BAM.

Mmm. Mmm. Mmm.

Wee. Wee. Wee!

The Three Bears cooked bowls of porridge. The porridge was hot so they went for a walk.

BAM. BAM. BAM.

Mmm. Mmm. Mmm.

Wee. Wee. Wee!

A pretty little girl named Goldie Locks was walking through the forest when she spied the Bears' house. She went to the window and caught a whiff of that porridge. It smelled yummy so she decided to go inside.

La dee da. La dee da.

At the table, she saw three bowls of porridge. The first bowl of porridge was BIG. The second bowl of porridge was small. The third bowl of porridge looked just right so Goldie Locks took a great big bite.

Too big, too small.

Just right, now bite!

La dee da. La dee da.

She loved the porridge so much that she gobbled it all up.

55

After eating the yummy porridge, Goldie Locks wanted to relax. She went into the living room and saw three chairs. The first chair was BIG. The second chair was small. The third chair looked just right, so Goldie Locks squeezed in tight.

Too big, too small.

Just right, sit tight.

La dee da. La dee da.

But the third chair CRACKED and Goldie Locks broke it, just like that.

So Goldie Locks explored the cabin and saw three beds. The first bed was BIG! The second bed was small. The third bed looked just right so Goldie Locks snuggled in tight.

Too big, too small.

Just right, sleep tight!

La dee da. La dee da.

As soon as Goldie Locks laid down her head, she fell asleep in the third bed. Meanwhile, the three Bears were on their way home.

BAM. BAM. BAM.

Mmm. Mmm. Mmm.

Wee. Wee. Wee!

When they arrived home, they saw the table. Oh no! Baby Bear cried, "Papa, Mama, my porridge is gone! Wee wee wee!"

They went into the living room and saw their chairs. Baby Bear cried, "Papa, Mama, my chair is broken! Wee wee wee!"

They went into their rooms and saw their beds. Baby Bear cried, "Papa, Mama, my bed is full! Wee wee wee!"

Goldie Locks heard the ruckus and opened her eyes. Imagine her surprise!

Papa Bear said, "You didn't have to eat all of Baby Bear's porridge! BAM! BAM! BAM!"

Mama Bear said, "You didn't have to break Baby Bear's chair! Mmm. Mmm. Mmm."

And Baby Bear said, "You didn't have to sleep in my bed! Wee. Wee. Wee!"

Well Goldie Locks jumped up lickety-split and jumped out of the window.

La dee da. La dee da.

La dee da. La dee da.

The three Bears never saw Goldie Locks again and you can be sure that Goldie Locks NEVER again touched anything that didn't belong to her.

La. Dee. Da!

Hansel and Gretel

Germany

Once upon a time, there was a woodcutter who lived with his wife and two children, a brave boy named Hansel and a sweet girl named Gretel. The woodcutter's wife was their stepmother and she did not like the children. They were poor and had barely enough food to feed the four of them.

The woodcutter cried, "What are we to do? I can scarcely put food in my children's mouths!"

The wife answered, "If we did not have children, it would not be a problem. We would have plenty enough food for the both of us."

The woodcutter said, "But I do have children and I must feed them."

The wife said, "If we don't do something soon, we will all die of starvation. Let us take the children into the woods and leave them there. They will never find their way back and we will have enough food for our mouths alone."

"I cannot do that!" cried the woodcutter.

But the evil woman had a way of persuading the woodcutter to follow her fiendish plan. Neither the woodcutter nor his wicked wife knew that Hansel and Gretel heard the entire conversation. Gretel began to cry. "What is to become of us, brother?"

Hansel answered, "Do not fret, dear Gretel. I have a plan." He stole out the back door and filled his pockets with white pebbles that glittered like silver pieces in the moonlight.

The next morning, before the sun rose, the wife awoke the sleeping children. "Get up you lazy things. We are going into the forest to chop wood with your father." She gave each of them a piece of bread. "This is for your supper. Do not eat it before then. You shall receive nothing else."

Gretel filled her apron with the bread while Hansel filled his pockets with the pebbles. As they traveled farther into the forest, Hansel dropped the white pebbles along the way. When they came to the middle of the wood, the woodcutter built a fire.

The wife said, "Children, you stay here and rest while we go into the forest to chop wood. When we are ready, we will call for you." The woodcutter and his wife left Hansel and Gretel alone.

When it was time, the children ate their bread and then fell asleep. When they awoke, the fire was burned out and the moon rose high in the sky. Gretel began to cry, "They have left us and we are all alone."

Hansel comforted his sister. "Do not fret, dear Gretel. We have a way back home." He pointed to the white pebbles that glittered like silver pieces in the moonlight. They followed the pebbles and found their way home.

When they knocked on the door, the wife answered. She cried, "There you are, you wicked little children! We called and you never came. We thought you were never coming home again." But their father was glad because it broke his heart to leave his children all alone in the woods.

Soon after, bread was again scarce in the household. The woodcutter cried, "What are we to do? I can barely put food in my children's mouths!"

The wife answered, "If we did not have children, it would not be a problem. We would have plenty enough food for the both of us."

The woodcutter said, "But I do have children and I must feed them."

The wife said, "If we don't do something soon, we will all die of starvation. Let us take the children into the woods once more and leave them there. We will take them deep into the forest, where they have never been. They will never find their way back and we will have enough food for our mouths alone."

"I cannot do that!" cried the woodcutter.

But the evil woman had a way of persuading the woodcutter to follow her fiendish plan. Neither the woodcutter nor his wicked wife knew that Hansel and Gretel heard the entire conversation again. Gretel began to cry. "What is to become of us, brother?"

Hansel answered, "Do not fret, dear Gretel. I have a plan." He tried to sneak out the back door to collect pebbles but found that the door was barred tight.

The next morning, before the sun rose, the wife awoke the sleeping children. "Get up you lazy things. We are going into the forest to chop wood with your father." She gave each of them a piece of bread, even smaller than the pieces she had previously given them. "This is for your supper. Do not eat it before then. You shall receive nothing else."

Gretel filled her apron with one piece of bread while Hansel filled his pockets with the crumbs of the other. As they traveled farther into the forest, Hansel dropped the bread crumbs along the way. They traveled even farther into the woods to a place the children had never been. When they came to the middle of the dark forest, the wood-cutter built a fire.

The wife said, "Children, you stay here and rest while we go into the forest to chop wood. When we are ready, we will call for you." The woodcutter and his wife left Hansel and Gretel alone.

When it was time, the children shared the single piece of bread and then fell asleep. When they awoke, the fire was burned out and the moon rose high in the sky. Gretel began to cry, "They have left us and we are all alone."

Hansel comforted his sister. "Do not fret, dear Gretel. We have a way back home." He pointed to the trail of breadcrumbs. But there was no trail, for thousands of birds had pecked and picked them up.

Hansel said, "I will find a way, Gretel. Follow me." The two children walked through the night and into the day when finally they came upon a cottage. What a wondrous cottage it was, for its walls were made of gingerbread, its roof was made of frosted cake, and its windows were made of clear sugar.

"There," Hansel pointed. "We shall have a glorious feast!"

The children ran to the house and began nibbling. Hansel grabbed a handful of the gingerbread wall. Gretel bit into the clear sugar window.

A sweet voice called from inside the house,

"Nibbling, Nibbling like a mouse
Who is nibbling at my house?"
The children answered,
"The wind, the wind blows at your house
Blowing north and blowing south."

Hansel and Gretel continued eating. This time, Hansel bit into the clear sugar window and Gretel grabbed a handful of the gingerbread wall.

The sweet voice called again from inside the house,

"Nibbling, Nibbling like a mouse
Who is nibbling at my house?"
The children answered,
"The wind, the wind blows at your house
Blowing north and blowing south."

The sweet voice belonged to an old woman and she came outside to see Hansel and Gretel nibbling at her house. The children were frightened but the old woman was kind.

"Come inside for a bite to eat
Pancakes and milk are such a treat."

They followed the old woman inside the house. They ate until they were stuffed and fell asleep in soft beds, thinking they were in heaven. Ah, but they were terribly deceived for the old woman was really an old witch with wicked intentions. She built her house of sweets to entice children inside. Once she trapped the children, they became her . . . dinner!

When Hansel and Gretel awoke, she locked Hansel in a cage and ordered Gretel to fetch some water to cook something good for her brother to eat.

The old witch said,

"The little boy will eat, eat, eat

He'll grow fat and be MY treat!"

Gretel cooked a fine meal for Hansel but she herself was fed nothing but crab claw shells.

Each morning, the witch came to the cage and had Hansel stretch out his finger saying,

"By now you should be growing fat

You'll be my meal and that is that!"

But Hansel was clever. The witch had poor eyesight and each time she came to the cage, he stuck out a chicken bone for her to feel.

After a long month passed, the witch grew impatient.

"Be he skinny or be he fat

I'll eat him NOW and that is that!"

She ordered Gretel to put on a pot of boiling water. Intending to cook Gretel too, she said,

"Into the oven place your head

Is it hot enough for my bread?"

But Gretel was a clever girl. She answered,

"I am a simple child now

Please take me there and show me how."

So the witch took Gretel to the oven and opened it up. She placed her head inside the oven and as soon as she did, Gretel pushed the witch inside and then locked the door tight. How the witch screamed. How the witch howled. But it was no use. Turning to ash, she met her fate in the heat of the oven.

Gretel unlocked Hansel's cage and the two embraced. With the witch now gone, they searched the house and found pearls and jewels. Gretel filled her apron with the pearls while Hansel filled his pockets with the jewels.

They broke off pieces of the sweet cottage for their supper and began their journey home. Soon enough, they saw a familiar house in the distance. They ran and knocked on the door. Their father answered. Filled with joy, he embraced his children saying he would never, never again leave them alone. As for their wicked stepmother, like the evil witch, she too met an awful fate and died when a pile of wood fell atop her head.

Gretel shook her apron and the pearls rolled out onto the floor. Hansel emptied his pockets and the jewels sparkled on the table. All their sorrows were ended and they lived together in great happiness.

Little mouse, little mouse, run, run, run.

This story's over; my tale is done.

Henny Penny

England

One day, Henny Penny was clucking along when an acorn fell on her head. "Ouch!" she yelled. She reached up and felt a lump. When she looked up, she saw the sky. She cried,

The sky is falling! The sky is falling! It's a terrible thing!

Hurry up! Hurry up! I must go tell the king!

Along the way, Henny Penny met Rooster Looster. Rooster Looster asked, "Where are you going?" Henny Penny cried,

The sky is falling! The sky is falling! It's a terrible thing!

Hurry up! Hurry up! We must go tell the king!

Along the way, Henny Penny and Rooster Looster met Ducky Lucky. Ducky Lucky asked, "Where are you going?" They cried,

The sky is falling! The sky is falling! It's a terrible thing!

Hurry up! Hurry up! We must go tell the king!

Along the way, Henny Penny, Rooster Looster, and Ducky Lucky met Goosey Loosey. Goosey Loosey asked, "Where are you going?" They cried,

The sky is falling! The sky is falling! It's a terrible thing!

Hurry up! Hurry up! We must go tell the king!

Along the way, Henny Penny, Rooster Looster, Ducky Lucky, and Goosey Loosey met Turkey Lurkey. Turkey Lurkey asked, "Where are you going?" They cried,

The sky is falling! The sky is falling! It's a terrible thing!

Hurry up! Hurry up! We must go tell the king!

Along the way, Henny Penny, Rooster Looster, Ducky Lucky, Goosey Loosey, and Turkey Lurkey met Foxy Loxy. Foxy Loxy asked, "Where are you going?" They cried,

63

The sky is falling! The sky is falling! It's a terrible thing!

Hurry up! Hurry up! We must go tell the king!

Foxy Loxy's stomach grumbled and he licked his lips. "Dinner!" he thought to himself. Foxy Loxy said, "That is not the way to the king. I will show you the way. Follow me." So Henny Penny, Rooster Looster, Ducky Lucky, Goosey Loosey, and Turkey Lurkey followed Foxy Loxy.

Henny Penny, Rooster Looster, Ducky Lucky, Goosey Loosey, and Turkey Lurkey followed Foxy Loxy to a dark cave. Foxy Loxy said, "The king is in there." So everyone walked into the cave. Henny Penny said, "I don't see the king." Foxy Loxy said, licking his lips, "I am the king now and I am about to have my royal dinner!" Just then, they heard loud barking nearby.

It was the king's hound dog. Foxy Loxy ran out of the cave with the dog chasing close behind. Henny Penny, Rooster Looster, Ducky Lucky, Goosey Loosey, and Turkey Lurkey escaped and ran back home. From that time on, Henny Penny decided that if the sky ever fell again, she would keep it to herself!

The sky is falling! The sky is falling! It's a terrible thing!

Shhh. Be quiet. Shhh. Be quiet. I won't go tell the king!

Jack and the Beanstalk

England

There was once a poor widow who had an only son named Jack. They had a cow named Milky-White. All they had to live on was the milk the cow provided each morning and the money they made from selling the milk at the market. But one morning, Milky-White gave no more milk.

"A terrible fate has befallen us! What are we to do?" cried the old widow. She wrung her hands and tapped her foot nervously. Suddenly, an idea came.

"I know!" she cried. "We shall sell Milky-White!"

Jack said, "I'll take the cow to the market and sell her."

Jack's mother said, "Don't do anything foolish, Jack. Sell Milky-White and we will be alright."

Jack nodded and led the cow down the road. It wasn't long before they met a man on the side of the road.

The man tipped his hat. "Good day, young lad," he said to Jack. "Where are you headed on this fine morning?"

Jack answered, "I am going to the market to sell our bonny cow."

The man said, "Well look no further! I have a deal for you, which you cannot refuse! I will trade you your bonny cow for the contents of this small purse." The man shook a small leather pouch. "What is inside is worth more than fifteen milk-giving cows!"

"What is it?" Jack asked, his curiosity growing.

"Ah," said the man, "inside this bag awaits your future!"

"What do you mean?" asked Jack, scratching his head.

65

From *Stories on Board! Creating Board Games from Favorite Tales* by Dianne de Las Casas. Illustrated by Soleil Lisette. Santa Barbara, CA: Libraries Unlimited. Copyright © 2010.

"Inside this bag is a handful of magic beans. If you plant them overnight, by morning, a stalk shall grow right up to the sky, to the Land of the Great Beyond, where riches abound!"

Jack's excitement grew. "Yes, I'll do it!" he exclaimed. "I shall trade Milky-White for your magic beans." And so, the deal was made. Jack walked home with a small leather pouch full of beans.

When he arrived home, his mother asked excitedly, "I see that you come home with no cow. You must have sold Milky-White! What did you get for her?"

Jack held the leather pouch in front of him. "Mama, I traded our bonny cow for these magic beans!"

The old woman's eyes grew wide. "You did what?!" she cried. She snatched the leather pouch, untied the string, and poured the beans out into her palm.

"Oh Jack! You are but a fool. These are no magic beans. You have been swindled. Now we have nothing!" She tossed the beans out the window and said, "Not a sip shall you drink and not a bit shall you swallow tonight. Leave me be."

Jack went to his room and fell asleep with his tummy rumbling loudly. Just as the sun's rays touched Jack's window, Jack's eyes flew open. Something was amiss! He opened his eyes wide to discover that a large beanstalk had grown overnight and climbed into the sky, just as the man had promised.

"I shall make it up to mother and travel to this Land of the Great Beyond and bring her back the riches she deserves." Jack began ascending the beanstalk, one foot above the other. When he reached the top, he followed a road that led him to a great big house. On the doorstep was a great big woman.

"Good morning, mum," he said ever so politely. "Would you be so kind as to give me some breakfast? My tummy rumbles loudly and I have not had a sip of drink nor a bit to swallow in quite some time."

The great big woman was the wife of a great big ogre. She had a soft spot for little boys. "Oh alright. I will feed you but make haste for my husband does not like boys. If you hear him, hide in the oven."

No sooner had Jack finished his meal when he heard, "THUD. THUD. THUD."

Jack jumped into the oven and hid. The great big ogre sat at the table. "Wife, I am so hungry I could eat a horse." He tossed her a horse and said, "Cook it."

Jack's eyes grew wide as the ogre began sniffing the air.

"Fee Fi Fo Fum.

I smell the blood of an Englishman.

Be he alive or be he dead,

I'll grind his bones to make my bread."

The ogre's wife said, "I am sure you are just imagining things. Why don't you take a nap?"

The ogre grunted and left the table. Jack was just about to run away when the great big woman said, "Wait until he is asleep to sneak out."

So Jack waited. The ogre went to a big chest and brought out three bags of gold. Holding the gold, he began snoring.

On tiptoe, Jack crept out of the oven and carefully pried one of the bags of gold from the ogre's arm. Then he ran all the way to the beanstalk and climbed down as fast as his legs could carry him. He showed his mother the gold and told her the story. She was pleased and they lived off the gold for some time but finally, they came to the end of it. Jack said, "I will climb again."

Jack began ascending the beanstalk, one foot above the other. When he reached the top, he followed a road that led him to a great big house. Again on the doorstep, was a great big woman.

"Good morning, mum," he said ever so politely. "Would you be so kind as to give me some breakfast? My tummy rumbles loudly and I have not had a sip of drink nor a bit to swallow in quite some time."

The great big woman was the wife of a great big ogre. She narrowed her eyes. "Aren't you the lad that came and left the same day a bag of my husband's gold went missing?"

Jack answered, "I don't know much about anything, mum, because I am so hungry. Please take pity and feed me."

"Oh alright. I will feed you but make haste for my husband does not like boys. If you hear him, hide in the oven."

No sooner had Jack finished his meal when he heard, "THUD. THUD. THUD."

Jack jumped into the oven and hid. The great big ogre sat at the table. "Wife, I am so hungry I could eat a cow." He tossed her a cow and said, "Cook it."

Jack's eyes grew wide as the ogre began sniffing the air.

"Fee Fi Fo Fum.

I smell the blood of an Englishman.

Be he alive or be he dead,

I'll grind his bones to make my bread."

The ogre's wife said, "I am sure you are just imagining things. Why don't you take a nap?"

The ogre grunted and left the table. Jack was just about to run away when the great big woman said, "Wait until he is asleep to sneak out."

So Jack waited. The ogre went into a room and brought out a golden hen. Holding the hen, he said, "Lay," and it laid an egg made of solid gold. Soon after, the ogre began snoring.

On tiptoe, Jack crept out of the oven and carefully picked up the hen. The hen squawked but Jack ran all the way to the beanstalk and climbed down as fast as his legs could carry him. He showed his mother the golden hen and told her the story. She was pleased and they lived off the golden eggs for some time but Jack grew restless. Jack said, "I will climb again."

Jack began ascending the beanstalk, one foot above the other. When he reached the top, he followed a road that led him to a great big house. He knew better than to confront the great big woman so he snuck into the house. No sooner had he hidden in the oven when he heard, "THUD. THUD. THUD."

The great big ogre sat at the table. "Wife, I am so hungry I could eat an elephant." He tossed her an elephant and said, "Cook it."

Jack's eyes grew wide as the ogre began sniffing the air.

"Fee Fi Fo Fum.

I smell the blood of an Englishman.

Be he alive or be he dead,

I'll grind his bones to make my bread."

The ogre's wife said, "I am sure you are just imagining things. There is no one here. Why don't you take a nap? I shall fetch your golden harp to sing you to sleep."

The ogre grunted and left the table. Jack waited. The great big woman brought the ogre his golden harp. He ordered, "Sing."

The harp sang most beautifully and sang until the ogre began snoring.

On tiptoe, Jack crept out of the oven and carefully picked up the golden harp. But the harp cried out, "Master! Master!"

The giant ogre awoke with a roar. "Stop you little thief. I shall grind your bones when I get a hold of you!"

Jack sprinted all the way to the beanstalk with the golden harp in tow. He climbed down as fast as his legs could carry him.

But the ogre did not give up easily. He too began lumbering down the beanstalk. When Jack reached the bottom, he yelled, "Mother, mother! Get me the axe!"

Jack handed the harp to his mother and took the axe from her. He began furiously chopping down the thick stalk.

"Thunk, thunk, thunk, thunk, thunk!" The stalk began to sway and though the ogre tried to climb back up, it was all in vain. The beanstalk began to shiver and shake. Then it fell to the ground with a very loud THUD, killing the ogre instantly.

Jack showed his mother the golden harp, which now called Jack, "Master." With the golden hen and the golden harp, Jack gave his mother all the riches she deserved. Jack went to bed every night with a sip of drink, a bit to swallow, and a very full belly. And they lived happily ever after.

Jack Seeks His Fortune

England

In a land of green rolling hills, there once lived a boy named Jack. One day, Jack decided that it was time for him to make his fortune. He began traveling down the road. He had not gone very far when he met a sad old donkey. The donkey said:

Hee haw, I don't know what to do.

My master doesn't want me—can I go with you?

Jack said, "Sure!" And off the two traveled. They journeyed down the road a little ways when they met a sad old cow. The cow said:

Moo moo, I don't know what to do.

My master doesn't want me—can I go with you?

Jack said, "Sure!" And off the three traveled. They journeyed down the road a little ways when they met a sad old dog. The dog said:

Arf arf, I don't know what to do.

My master doesn't want me—can I go with you?

Jack said, "Sure!" And off the four traveled. They journeyed down the road a little ways when they met a sad old cat. The cat said:

Meow meow, I don't know what to do.

My master doesn't want me—can I go with you?

Jack said, "Sure!" And off the five traveled. They journeyed down the road a little ways when they met a sad old rooster. The rooster said:

Cock-a-doodle-do, I don't know what to do.

My master doesn't want me—can I go with you?

Jack said, "Sure!" And off they all traveled. They journeyed until it was nearly dark. Then Jack spotted a house. He told the animals, "Ssssshhhh" as he peeked in

69

through the window. Much to his surprise, he saw a gang of robbers counting their gold!

Jack had a bright idea. He said, "When I wave my hand, make as much noise as you can." When the animals were ready, Jack gave the signal. The donkey brayed, the cow mooed, the dog barked, the cat meowed, and the rooster crowed. Together, they made such an awful racket that the noise scared away the robbers and they left behind all of their—gold!

Jack and the animals went inside the house and got comfortable. Then Jack began to worry that the robbers would come back. So he came up with another plan. He put the donkey near the door, the cow by the fireplace, the dog under the table, the cat in the rocking chair, and the rooster on a beam at the top. Finally, Jack fell asleep.

Jack was right. The robbers returned. They decided to look for their gold. They sent one of their men inside the house. When the robber came in, the rooster crowed loudly, the cat scratched him, the dog bit his leg, the cow slapped him with his tail, and the donkey kicked him out the door. He ran back to the other robbers and they never returned to the house again.

Jack and the animals had themselves a nice house and a big pile of—gold! They lived there in peace and contentment for the rest of their days. Jack made his fortune, but the best fortune of all was his friends.

The Lion and the Mouse

Aesop Fable from Greece

Ssssshh. In the jungle the lion was sleeping. He was taking a nap. By and by, a little mouse, not watching where she was walking, stepped on the lion's nose and woke him up. He ROARED!

He wrapped his paws around the little mouse and said, "You should never wake a lion from his cat nap." The little mouse said, "I'm sorry, Mr. Lion. If you let me go, I promise to be your friend and help you when you are in need. Please let me go."

But the lion shook his head no and wouldn't let go.

The lion said, "You! Friend to a great beast like myself! Ha! Never!" The mouse said again, "Please, Mr. Lion, I can be your friend. Let me go."

But the lion shook his head no and wouldn't let go.

So the little mouse did something different. She began to whine. "Pleeeeeeease let me goooooooooooooooo." She was making such a racket that the Lion let go and covered both of his ears with his paws. The little mouse scampered off.

A few days later, the little mouse was walking through the jungle when she heard a strange noise. It sounded like a sick kitty cat moaning and groaning.

Meow. Meow. Moan. Groan.

The lion was caught in a hunter's net. When the lion saw the mouse, he begged for help. The little mouse said, "I made a promise and I will keep it. But if I help you and set you free, you must promise not to EAT me!" The lion promised.

The little mouse nibbled and nibbled through the net until the lion was free. He stood up and let out a ferocious ROAR!

From *Stories on Board! Creating Board Games from Favorite Tales* by Dianne de Las Casas. Illustrated by Soleil Lisette. Santa Barbara, CA: Libraries Unlimited. Copyright © 2010.

Then he reached for the mouse and without saying a word pulled her close to his mouth. She cried out, "You promised not to eat me!" Suddenly, the lion bent down and gave the mouse a great big SMOOCH on the lips.

From that time forward, the Lion and the Mouse were the best of friends, and it just goes to show you that friendship comes in all shapes and sizes.

The Little Red Hen

England

Twice as long as long ago, there lived a little red hen. She was looking for some food in the farmyard when she found some grains of wheat. She saw her friends and asked, "Now who will help me plant the wheat?"

"Not I," said the Dog.

"Not I," said the Cat.

"Not I," said the Duck.

And that was that.

"Then I'll plant it myself," and she did.

When the wheat grew tall, the little red hen asked her friends, "Now who will help me cut the wheat?"

"Not I," said the Dog.

"Not I," said the Cat.

"Not I," said the Duck.

And that was that.

"Then I'll cut it myself," and she did.

When the wheat was cut, the little red hen asked her friends, "Now who will help me grind the wheat?"

"Not I," said the Dog.

"Not I," said the Cat.

"Not I," said the Duck.

And that was that.

"Then I'll grind it myself," and she did.

When the wheat was ground, the little red hen asked her friends, "Now who will help me bake the bread?"

"Not I," said the Dog.

"Not I," said the Cat.

"Not I," said the Duck.

And that was that.

"Then I'll bake it myself," and she did.

When the bread was baked, the little red hen asked her friends, "Now who will help me eat the bread?"

"I will," said the Dog.

"I will," said the Cat.

"I will," said the Duck.

And that was that.

"Oh no, you won't," said the little red hen.

"None of you helped me plant the wheat, cut the wheat, grind the wheat, or bake the bread! I'll eat it myself!" And she did!

Little Red Riding Hood

Germany

Deep, deep, way deep in the woods, there lived a pretty little girl who was loved by everyone, especially her Granny.

The little girl's mother called her over and gave her a beautiful red cape with a hood. The girl was so fond of it that she wore it all the time. So she became known as Little Red Riding Hood.

One day, her mother called, "Little Red Riding Hood!"

Little Red Riding Hood listened to her mother and came at once. "Yes, Mama, what is it?"

Mama handed Little Red Riding Hood a big basket from which delicious aromas floated through the air. The basket was filled with freshly baked bread and homemade jam. Her mother said, "This is for Granny. I need you to deliver this gift."

Little Red Riding Hood said,

"Freshly baked bread and homemade jam

I am Red Riding Hood, yes I am!"

Mama said, "Yes, but listen, my child. Hurry and bring it to her, quick, quick, quick. Be careful and don't stop along the way."

"Yes, Mama," said Little Red Riding Hood and she set out for her grandmother's house.

Granny lived deep, deep, way deep in the woods, far from Little Red Riding Hood's house. It was a long walk. By and by, she came upon a big wolf. She did not know what a malicious beast he was so she was not at all afraid. "Hello, Wolf."

"How are you, Little Red Riding Hood?" the big wolf responded. "Where are you headed to with that big basket?"

"Oh, I am going to my Granny's house to deliver a gift."

"Freshly baked bread and homemade jam
I am Red Riding Hood, yes I am!"

"It seems so much that a little girl like you should be carrying such a heavy basket. Perhaps I could help you," said the big wolf, grinning mischievously.

"That's okay, Wolf. I am strong. I can carry it by myself. Granny's house is only a quarter mile ahead. Thank you." And Little Red Riding Hood skipped in the direction of her grandmother's house.

But the crafty and cunning wolf showed Little Red Riding Hood a beautiful bouquet of blossoms. "Wouldn't your grandmother love these flowers?" he asked.

Little Red Riding Hood answered, "You are right. I think Granny would love some of these flowers to set on the table."

So the wolf began to bargain. "I'll give you these beautiful flowers in exchange for your pretty red riding hood. My ears are always exposed and your red riding hood would keep them warm."

The wolf made puppy eyes at Little Red Riding Hood and she said, "Very well." So she traded her bonnet for the flowers and tromped deeper into the woods, while the cunning wolf dashed ahead to her grandmother's house. When he arrived at Granny's house, he knocked on the door.

"Who is it?" yelled Granny.

"It's me, Little Red Riding Hood. I've come to deliver a gift." answered the wolf, trying to disguise his voice.

"Freshly baked bread and homemade jam
I am Red Riding Hood, yes I am!"

"Then come on in, Little Red Riding Hood. Granny has missed you."

The wolf opened the door and entered the house. As soon as Granny saw him, she bolted out of bed and ran to the door. But it was too late. The big wolf caught her and gobbled her down in one gulp. He then put on her apron and her bonnet and hopped into bed, waiting for Little Red Riding Hood.

By and by, Little Red Riding Hood knocked on the door.

"Who is it?" yelled the wolf, disguising his voice to sound like Granny.

"It's me, Little Red Riding Hood. I've come to deliver a gift," answered Little Red Riding Hood.

"Freshly baked bread and homemade jam
I am Red Riding Hood, yes I am!"

"Then come on in, Little Red Riding Hood. Granny has missed you."

Little Red Riding Hood opened the door and entered the house, setting the basket and a handful of flowers on the table. Little Red Riding Hood saw who she thought was Granny lying in bed.

She approached the bed and said, "Granny what great ears you have."

The wolf answered, "The better to hear you with, my dear."

"And Granny, what great eyes you have."

The wolf answered, "The better to see you with, my dear."

"And Granny, what a great nose you have!"

The wolf answered, "The better to smell you with, my dear."

"And Granny, what great TEETH you have!"

The wolf answered, "The better to EAT you with, my dear!"

The words were scarcely out of his mouth when he sprang up out of bed, chasing Little Red Riding Hood.

Little Red Riding Hood was quick, quick, quick. She gave the wolf a good chase and finally bounded out the door. The wolf did not tire easily, he followed her out as Little Red Riding Hood cried, "Help! Help!"

It just so happened that a nearby woodsman heard Little Red Riding Hood's cries for help. He ran to Little Red Riding Hood and just in the nick of time, he caught the wolf with his bare hands, just before the wolf caught Little Red Riding Hood. With his strong arms, he knocked that wolf silly. Before you knew it, the woodsman reached down into the wolf's mouth and pulled out Granny. Then he took that puny old wolf and threw him deep into the woods. Granny was a little shaken up but none worse for the wear. And believe me, the wolf never bothered any of them again.

Granny and Little Red Riding Hood invited the woodsman over to share a little gift.

"Freshly baked bread and homemade jam

I am Red Riding Hood, yes I am!"

Deep, deep, way deep in the woods, a girl, a Granny, and a woodsman ate, drank, and rejoiced into the night.

And that my friends, is the very, very end.

Natasha and Baba Yaga

Russia

Once upon a time, on the other side of yesterday, there lived a mother and her daughter, Natasha. One day, Natasha's mother needed a needle and thread to mend the clothes.

She said to her daughter, "Natasha, I need you to visit the home of Baba Yaga, the wise woman of the forest. Please ask nicely to borrow a needle and thread."

Natasha had heard stories of Baba Yaga and they scared her. Baba Yaga was not a wise woman. She was, in fact, a wicked witch. She lived in a hut built on dancing chicken legs. She rode around in a mortar, steering with her pestle. Worst of all, she had teeth of metal and LOVED for children to be her . . . dinner!

Although Natasha was afraid, she was a dutiful daughter and always listened to her mother. Natasha's mother gave her a basket filled with a stick of butter, a piece of meat, and a hunk of bread. Natasha traveled long and far and finally reached Baba Yaga's hut on dancing chicken legs. The hut was behind a long fence with a great gate. When Natasha pushed through the gate, it creaked and moaned in agony.

Natasha said, "Poor gate. You need your hinges greased." She took out the stick of butter and rubbed it on the gate's hinges. It opened quietly and allowed Natasha to pass.

As Natasha walked up the path, she came upon a mangy, skinny dog in the yard. The dog growled. "Poor dog. You need some food." She took out the piece of meat and fed it to the dog. The dog gobbled it up quickly and appreciatively. He wagged his tail and allowed Natasha to pass.

A thin, scrawny cat sitting near the hut mewed pitifully. "Poor cat. You need some food." She took out the hunk of bread and fed it to the cat. The cat gobbled it up quickly and appreciatively. She purred and allowed Natasha to pass.

Baba Yaga sniffed the air. A child was present! She poked her head out of the window. "What do you want, little girl?" she asked as she licked her lips.

Natasha answered, "My mother has sent me to borrow a needle and thread."

"Come in then, child." The hut bent down and allowed Natasha inside.

Then Baba Yaga ordered, "Now get in the tub and wash yourself. I want you clean when I cook you for my dinner!" She grinned and her metal teeth flashed in the light. Baba Yaga locked Natasha in the bathroom.

Natasha began to cry. A voice spoke, "Do not cry, little girl. I will help you." It was the thin, scrawny cat. "You were kind to me and I am returning the favor. Fill the tub and splash around but don't get in."

Natasha nodded and did as she was instructed. She filled the tub with water and splashed.

Baba Yaga yelled through the door, "Are you washing yourself?"

Natasha answered,

"Splishy, splash

Splashy splish

I'm washing up

Just as you wish."

"Good." Baba Yaga went outside to collect wood for her stove.

While Baba Yaga was gone, the cat said, "Now take this mirror and comb. When you are in trouble, throw the mirror behind you. When you are in trouble again, throw the comb behind you. Now climb out the window."

Natasha thanked the cat and said, "But Baba Yaga will know I am gone when I do not answer her."

The cat said, "Do not worry. I will take care of Baba Yaga."

So Natasha ran as fast as her little legs would carry her. When she came to the dog in the yard, he happily gave Natasha a ride to the gate. The dog said, "You were kind to me and I am returning the favor."

When she came to the gate, the gate happily swung wide open for her. The gate said, "You were kind to me and I am returning the favor."

Meanwhile, Baba Yaga returned to the hut. She yelled through the bathroom door, "Are you washing yourself?"

The cat answered,

"Splishy splash

Splashy splish

I'm washing up

Just as you wish."

"Good." Baba Yaga went and lit the wood inside her stove. When she returned, she yelled through the bathroom door, "Are you washing yourself?"

The cat answered,
"Splishy splash
Splashy splish
I'm washing up
Just as you wish."

But Baba Yaga grew impatient. "You are taking too long. I shall cook you now." She flung open the door only to discover the cat bathing inside the tub.

Baba Yaga screamed, "Cat, why did you not stop the girl?"

The cat answered, "All these years you've been mean and only threw me scraps to eat. The little girl fed me well so I helped her."

Baba Yaga was angry. She ran outside and said to the dog in the yard, "Dog, why did you not stop the girl?"

The dog answered, "All these years you've been mean and only threw me scraps to eat. The little girl fed me well so I helped her."

Baba Yaga was furious. She ran all the way to the gate and screamed, "Gate, why did you not stop the girl?"

The gate answered, "All these years you've been mean and never once oiled my hinges. The little girl greased me well so I helped her."

Baba Yaga was enraged. She ran so fast that she nearly caught up to Natasha. Natasha looked behind her and saw Baba Yaga on her heels. She reached into her pocket and pulled out the mirror. She threw it behind her and a deep river formed between her and Baba Yaga.

Baba Yaga screamed, "I'll get you still!" Baba Yaga ran back to the house and hopped into her mortar. She floated across the river, using her pestle as an oar. Not only did her mortar float, it flew. Soon, Baba Yaga caught up to Natasha.

Natasha looked behind her and saw Baba Yaga flying on her heels. She reached into her pocket and pulled out the comb. She threw it behind her and a tall forest formed between her and Baba Yaga. In fact, the forest grew so tall that Baba Yaga could not even fly over it. Behind the cage of trees, Baba Yaga was trapped. She stomped her feet and pulled her hair.

Natasha ran all the way home into the arms of her mother. She told her mother the story and never again did Natasha have to borrow a needle and thread from the wicked and mean Baba Yaga.

Once upon a time, on the other side of yesterday, there lived a mother and her daughter, Natasha and they lived happily until the end of time.

Paul Bunyan and the Great Popcorn Blizzard

Tall Tale from the United States

Paul Bunyan was the mightiest logger in all of the North Woods. He was a giant man and he was so strong he could take a tree and snap it in half with his bare hands. His animal companion was Babe the Blue Ox and Paul headed a large logging camp.

When Paul chopped down the trees of North Dakota, he decided that it was time to head west. He and his men loaded their heavy equipment onto a boat that would travel down the Mississippi. It was going to be a long journey across the hot plains.

Paul and Babe the Blue Ox began leading the way west. Paul said to his men, "You better not get too thirsty because there isn't much water to be had along the hot plains."

On and on they trudged but the heat was too much. His men began to tire. Paul Bunyan's men said,

"We're baking in this sizzling heat.

We need to rest our weary feet!"

Hot Biscuit Slim, the camp's cook said, "I made us some vanilla ice cream but it's so hot that the ice cream began to boil!"

Paul Bunyan's men said,

"We're baking in this sizzling heat.

We need to rest our weary feet!"

But on they had to travel across the plains. Even Ole the Big Swede, who was the largest man in camp next to Paul, was growing tired. The men missed the cool shade of the tall trees. Paul Bunyan's men said,

"We're baking in this sizzling heat.

We need to rest our weary feet!"

Paul Bunyan himself became so tired that he began dragging his double-bitted axe behind him. The weight of the blade carved a ditch into the ground that became known as the Grand Canyon. Finally, it became so hot that the men refused to go any farther. Paul Bunyan's men said,

"We're baking in this sizzling heat.

We need to rest our weary feet!"

Hot Slim Biscuit said, "We're running out of food." So Paul went to the mountains. There, he found a farmer who had a barn full of corn. Paul bought the corn and brought it back to the men to feed them. But it was so hot that the corn began popping!

POP POP POP POP POP

POP POP POP POP POP

The popcorn fell to the ground like snowflakes. It covered the ground in white and Paul's men thought they were in the middle of a snow blizzard. In fact, they were so cold that they pulled out their coats, mittens, and scarves. They had to cover the horses in wool blankets so they would not freeze. They began making snow angels and having popcorn snowball fights. The popcorn snow kept falling.

POP POP POP POP POP

POP POP POP POP POP

The men were so happy to escape the heat and they were able to travel again. After traveling through the "snow," they finally reached the great forest in the West.

Only Paul and Babe the Blue Ox knew the truth. Whenever anyone would mention the "Great Snow Blizzard," Babe would wink and Paul would smile back.

POP POP POP POP POP

POP POP POP POP POP

Pecos Bill

United States

Pecos Bill was the greatest cowboy that ever lived. When he was just a baby, his daddy decided that he didn't like being crowded by the neighbors. So he took his 17 children, packed 'em in a wagon, and moved out west.

As Bill's family was crossing the Pecos River, Bill tumbled out. Since then, he has been known as Pecos Bill. His parents didn't discover he was gone until weeks later and by then, they figured it was too late. But Bill was a tough little feller and he was found by a coyote.

He grew up running with a pack of coyotes. Pecos Bill thought he was a coyote, too. One day, a man on a horse came riding by. It was quite a shock for the man to see Pecos Bill because Bill wasn't wearing any clothes.

The man asked, "Where are your clothes?"

Bill answered, "I'm a coyote and coyotes don't wear no clothes."

The cowboy said, "No you're not. You're a human."

Pecos Bill answered, "But I have fleas and I howl at night. That means I'm a coyote."

The cowboy laughed, "Everyone knows that all Texans have fleas and most of 'em howl at night. Coyotes have tails and you don't."

So the cowboy showed Bill that he had no tail and Pecos Bill realized his true nature. But living with coyotes all those years gave Pecos Bill some pretty special abilities and soon he became a rootin', tootin' cowboy.

Pecos Bill was from the Southwest.

There were other cowboys but he was the best.

85

When Pecos Bill was brought back to the ranch, the other cowboys made fun of him. They tried to trick Bill but they couldn't outwit him or outsmart him. Pecos Bill asked, "Who's the boss of this outfit?"

Gun Smith said, "I was but now you be the boss. You sure are a rootin', tootin' cowboy."

Pecos Bill was from the Southwest.

There were other cowboys but he was the best.

So Pecos Bill became the boss cowboy. He invented the lasso by using a 42-foot snake as a rope. Instead of buying a horse from town, Pecos Bill roped himself a wild, bucking bronco. His horse was named Lightning. Pecos Bill was so good at ropin' that he could snare a whole herd of cattle with one lariat. He was a rootin', tootin' cowboy.

Pecos Bill was from the Southwest.

There were other cowboys but he was the best.

Some say that Pecos Bill got tired of hauling in water from the Gulf of Mexico so one day, he dug the Grand Canyon. Pecos Bill was never thrown off the back of any animal—a cougar, a bear, or a horse. Why once, he even rode a cyclone bareback.

Pecos Bill threw his lariat and lassoed the cyclone by the neck. But the cyclone didn't take too kindly to Bill's presence. It lashed and snapped and twirled and whirled. For days, Bill tried to tame that tornado, but each was as stubborn as the other. He rode that cyclone over three states until he finally came down in California. That spot where Pecos Bill hog-tied that cyclone is known as Death Valley. He sure was a rootin', tootin' cowboy.

Pecos Bill was from the Southwest.

There were other cowboys but he was the best.

When Bill met Slue-Foot Sue, he fell head over spurs in love with her. One day, Slue-Foot Sue insisted on riding Lightning, Bill's horse. Now Lightning didn't let *anyone* ride him except Bill. As soon as Sue saddled up, Lightning bucked and sent Slue-Foot Sue sailing through the sky. Some say she bounced a few times on account of her hoop skirt but she never came back down.

How Pecos Bill met his end is still debated to this day. Some say he disappeared searching for Slue-Foot Sue. Others say he ate some barbed wire and it rusted his insides. Still others say he laughed himself to death one day. But there's one thing you can't dispute—Pecos Bill sure was a rootin', tootin' cowboy.

Pecos Bill was from the Southwest.

There were other cowboys but he was the best.

The Princess and the Bean

Denmark

There was once a Prince who wished to marry a Princess but she had to be a "real" Princess so he traveled around the whole world to find such a girl. There were Princesses aplenty but none of them satisfied his requirements. Something was always amiss. When he returned home, he was saddened, for his quest had gone unfulfilled.

One night, a terrible storm rose. As tines of lightning sliced the sky, there was a knock at the gate. Curious as to who could be traveling at this late hour in these dreadful conditions, the King himself went to open it.

A Princess stood outside the gate. What a state she was in. She looked like a drowned kitten; water ran down her disheveled clothes and out the toes of her muddied shoes. But she insisted that she was a real Princess.

The Queen received the young woman and said, "We'll soon find out." The Queen laid a small bean upon the floor and heaped 20 mattresses and 20 eider-down beds on top. There, the Princess was to sleep.

If the girl was indeed a real Princess, she would have to pass the test. A real princess would not be able to sleep.

In the morning, the Queen asked, "How was your sleep, dear?"

The Princess, looking exhausted and worn, said, "I do not mean to be rude, but I slept terribly. While I appreciate your hospitality, I could scarcely close my eyes the entire night. I do not know what was under the bed, but I lay upon something so hard that I am black and blue all over my body!"

It was evident, then, that she was a real Princess, since she had felt the bean through 20 mattresses and 20 eider-down beds. No one else could have so very fine a sense of feeling but a REAL Princess.

So the Prince and the Princess were married. The bean was placed in the Royal Museum, where it remains to this very day if no one has yet taken it away.

And this story is absolutely true. Mark my words!

Rapunzel

Germany

Once upon a time, there lived a man and his wife. They were poor people and could barely afford food. More than anything, they wished to have a child. But, alas, they wished in vain. The couple had a little window in the back of their house that overlooked a beautiful garden filled with fine flowers, fruit, and vegetables. The garden was surrounded by a high wall and no one dared to enter for it belonged to a witch who possessed great power.

One day, the woman was looking out her window into the garden when she spied the most green and leafy lettuce. It looked so fresh and colorful that a great desire filled her to eat one of these heads of lettuce. Every day she looked out of her window and longed for the lettuce. The wish tormented her daily and as she knew she could not have it, she became ill. She looked very pale and miserable.

Her husband, frightened by this, asked, "What ails you, my dear wife?"

She answered as she pointed out the window to the lettuce, "If I do not get any of that lettuce from that garden, I shall surely perish!"

The husband, who loved her very much, said, "I know that they belong to the witch but I will fetch you your lettuce, cost what they may!" So in the dark of the night, he climbed the wall of the witch's garden and snatched a head of lettuce.

He returned home to his wife, who made herself a giant salad with it. Having tasted the delicious lettuce, she longed for it even more. The next evening, her husband again climbed the wall, snatched a head of lettuce, and returned home. Once again, she made herself a lovely salad. Then she begged her husband for a third time to fetch more. The next evening, he proceeded to climb the wall but as he was snatching a head of lettuce, the old witch spied him.

89

"How dare you climb into my garden and steal my lettuce!"

The man cried, "Oh dear woman, please pardon me! I did this only out of necessity for my wife saw your lettuce from her window and took such a fancy to it that she surely would have perished had she not eaten it!"

The witch looked at the man and said, "Very well. Your wife will conceive. I will allow her lettuce every day if you promise me your newborn child."

The man was so anxious that he agreed. When his wife gave birth to a baby girl, the witch appeared and took away the child named Rapunzel, whose name means "lettuce."

Rapunzel grew to be such a beautiful young lady that the witch locked her away in a tall tower, which stood in a forest. It had neither stairs nor a door, only a little window at the top. Rapunzel was very lonely in the tower by herself. She had no one with whom to talk, dance, or tell stories. Only the witch came to visit and she wasn't very nice.

When the witch wished to enter the tower, she stood below on the ground and called out,

"Rapunzel, Rapunzel, I see you up there!

Rapunzel, Rapunzel, let down your hair!"

You see, Rapunzel had long and beautiful hair, as soft as silk, and as fine as spun gold. As soon as she heard the witch's cries, she let down her beautiful, thick braid, which served as a rope for the witch to climb up the tower.

One day, a young prince was riding through the wood. He heard a song so beautiful that he stood still and listened. It was Rapunzel singing.

"Trapped in this tower every day I see

The forest below and the sky above me.

Lonely and sad, I long for company.

Won't someone come and rescue me?"

The prince longed to soothe Rapunzel but could find no way to climb up into the tower. Every day, the prince would come to hear Rapunzel sing, but she never noticed him.

One day, the prince was watching Rapunzel and listening to her sing when he heard the witch call out,

"Rapunzel, Rapunzel, I see you up there!

Rapunzel, Rapunzel, let down your hair!"

Rapunzel let down her long braid and the witch climbed into the tower. The prince thought to himself, "That is how I must visit the lovely maiden!"

The prince went to the tower the next day and called out,

"Rapunzel, Rapunzel, I see you up there!

Rapunzel, Rapunzel, let down your hair!"

Rapunzel let down her long braid and the prince climbed into the tower. When Rapunzel saw him, she was frightened. The prince introduced himself to her and they began to talk. Soon, they were joking, laughing, and dancing.

He promised to come back the next day to visit Rapunzel, and he did. He called out,

"Rapunzel, Rapunzel, I see you up there!

Rapunzel, Rapunzel, let down your hair!"

Rapunzel let down her hair and the prince climbed up into the tower. Again, they laughed, talked, and danced. He brought her a gift. It was a book from which he read wonderful stories and showed her things she had never seen before.

Each time the prince came, he brought a skein of silk with him. Rapunzel wove the silk into an escape ladder until it was nearly ready. Then, one day the witch appeared below. She called out,

"Rapunzel, Rapunzel, I see you up there!

Rapunzel, Rapunzel, let down your hair!"

Rapunzel let down her hair and the witch climbed up into the tower. It was at that very moment that the prince happened to ride up to the tower. He did not know the witch was there and called out,

"Rapunzel, Rapunzel, I see you up there!

Rapunzel, Rapunzel, let down your hair!"

The prince was surprised to see the witch poke her head out of the tower window. The witch cried, "So young prince, you came to rescue Rapunzel? Here, rescue this!" The witch took a pair of scissors and in a great fury chopped off Rapunzel's beautiful hair. It fell into a heap on the ground below.

"Now you will never see her again, young prince!" the witch screamed.

It was then that Rapunzel turned to the witch, looked her straight in the eye, and with her back tall, said, "You cannot keep me here anymore. I am no longer your prisoner."

"And how do you suppose you are going to escape this tower now, Rapunzel?" the witch asked sarcastically.

"With cleverness and courage," Rapunzel answered. With that, she pulled out the silk ladder and rolled it out the window. Quickly, she climbed down. But the ladder wasn't quite finished. Hanging from the end, she jumped down straight into the prince's arms. Rapunzel and the prince pulled the ladder down and left the witch trapped in the tower, seething with anger.

Rapunzel and the prince mounted his horse and sped away. They never saw the witch again. Rapunzel and the prince were married and always had each other with whom to laugh, talk, share stories, and dance. And they lived happily ever after.

Sody Sallyraytus

Appalachian Mountains, United States

Once there lived a grandpa, a grandma, a little boy, a little girl, and their pet squirrel. One day, the grandma wanted to bake some biscuits but she was out of sody sallyraytus—baking soda. So she sent the little boy to the store. He bought the sody and sang a song home:

Sody sallyraytus, lickity-split

Grandma's going to bake some biscuits with it.

He started to cross the bridge but underneath the bridge lived a big, bad bully bear. The bear said, "I'll eat you up—you and your sody sallyraytus." And he did.

The little boy did not return home and Grandma said, "That boy is taking too long!" So she sent the little girl to the store. The little girl bought the sody and sang a song home.

Sody sallyraytus, lickity-split

Grandma's going to bake some biscuits with it.

She started to cross the bridge but underneath the bridge lived a big, bad bully bear. The bear said, "I ate the little boy. I'll eat you up too—you and your sody sally-raytus." And he did.

The little girl did not return home and Grandma said, "That girl is taking too long!" So she sent Grandpa to the store. Grandpa bought the sody and sang a song home.

Sody sallyraytus, lickity split

Grandma's going to bake some biscuits with it.

He started to cross the bridge but underneath the bridge lived a big, bad bully bear. The bear said, "I ate the little boy, I ate the little girl, and I'll eat you up too. You and your sody sallyraytus." And he did.

Grandpa did not return home and Grandma said, "That old man is taking too long! I'll fetch it myself." So she went to the store. She bought the sody and sang a song home.

Sody sallyraytus, lickity split
Grandma's going to bake some biscuits with it.

She started to cross the bridge but underneath the bridge there lived a big, bad bully bear. The bear said, "I ate the little boy, I ate the little girl, I ate the old man, and I'll eat you up too. You and your sody sallyraytus." And he did.

Now the pet squirrel was home by himself getting hungrier and hungrier. He went to the store. The storekeeper said the little boy, the little girl, the grandpa, and the grandma had all been there to buy sody sallyraytus. So the squirrel started home.

He began crossing the bridge but underneath the bridge there lived a big, bad bully bear. The bear said, "I ate the little boy, I ate the little girl, I ate the old man, I ate the old woman, and I'll eat you up too!"

"Oh no you won't!" said the little squirrel and lickity-split, he ran up a nearby tree. The big, bad bully bear began climbing that tree and following the squirrel. He growled, "If you can do it with your little legs, then I can do it with my big legs!"

But the branch could not bear the big, bad bully bear and it broke. Dooooooww-wwn he fell. THUD! Well, that bear fell so hard that out bounced the little boy, the little girl, Grandma, and Grandpa. And they each still had their sody sallyraytus. They all sang a song home.

Sody sallyraytus, lickity split
Grandma's going to bake some biscuits with it.
And she did. Squirrel sang happily
Mmm, mmm, mmm
Yummy in my tummy
The biscuits Grandma made us
From sody sallyraytus.

The Three Billy Goats Gruff

Norway

Long ago, there once lived three billy goats called the Three Billy Goats Gruff: Little Billy Goat Gruff, Middle Billy Goat Gruff, and BIG Billy Goat Gruff.

The three Billy Goats Gruff lived on one side of a canyon. Over the canyon was a bridge. Underneath the bridge lived a Hairy Scary Troll! No one wanted to cross the bridge because everyone was afraid of the . . . Hairy Scary Troll!

One day, Little Billy Goat Gruff looked across the canyon and on the other side, he saw sweet green grass. He wanted to eat some of that sweet green grass so he crossed the bridge like this:

Trip Trap Trip Trap

Trippity Trippity Trap

Just then, from underneath the bridge appeared the . . . Hairy Scary Troll!

The Hairy Scary Troll said, "Who's trippity trapping over my bridge?"

Little Billy Goat Gruff answered, "It is I, Little Billy Goat Gruff."

The troll said, "Little Billy Goat Gruff, you look tasty and I'm going to eat you up!"

Little Billy Goat Gruff said, "You don't want to eat me. I'm too small. Wait for my big brother, Middle Billy Goat Gruff. He is bigger than me and he will fill your belly."

"Fine," said the troll. "You may pass."

So Little Billy Goat Gruff crossed the bridge again, like this:

Trip Trap Trip Trap

Trippity Trippity Trap

Middle Billy Goat Gruff looked across the canyon and saw Little Billy Goat Gruff eating the sweet green grass. Middle Billy Goat Gruff wanted to eat some of that sweet green grass too so he crossed the bridge like this:

95

Trip Trap Trip Trap

Trippity Trippity Trap

Just then, from underneath the bridge appeared the . . . Hairy Scary Troll!

The Hairy Scary Troll said, "Who's trippity trapping over my bridge?"

Middle Billy Goat Gruff answered, "It is I, Middle Billy Goat Gruff."

The troll said, "Middle Billy Goat Gruff, you look tasty and I'm going to eat you up!"

Middle Billy Goat Gruff said, "You don't want to eat me. I'm too small. Wait for my big brother, BIG Billy Goat Gruff. He is bigger than me and he will fill your belly."

"Fine," said the troll. "You may pass."

So Middle Billy Goat Gruff crossed the bridge again, like this:

Trip Trap Trip Trap

Trippity Trippity Trap

Now BIG Billy Goat Gruff looked across the canyon and saw his two little brothers eating the sweet green grass. BIG Billy Goat Gruff wanted to eat some of that sweet green grass too so he crossed the bridge like this:

Trip Trap Trip Trap

Trippity Trippity Trap

Just then, from underneath the bridge appeared the . . . Hairy Scary Troll!

The Hairy Scary Troll said, "Who's trippity trapping over my bridge?"

BIG Billy Goat Gruff answered, "It is I, BIG Billy Goat Gruff."

The troll said, "BIG Billy Goat Gruff, you look tasty and I'm going to eat you up!"

"I don't think so!" said BIG Billy Goat Gruff. He bent down his BIG Billy Goat horns and charged at the Hairy Scary Troll. They collided and the troll flew up and then fell over the side of the bridge.

From that time forward, the three Billy Goats Gruff never heard from that Hairy Scary Troll ever again. They crossed the bridge whenever they pleased, like this:

Trip Trap Trip Trap

Trippity Trippity Trap

The Three Little Pigs

England

Once upon a time when the swine spoke rhyme, there were three little pigs. It was time for the three little pigs to leave their mama's house and build homes of their own. So Mama Bacon said, "Be sure to build strong homes. And beware of the big bad wolf!" She kissed each of her little piggies and sent them off into the world.

Now the first little pig saw a straw seller by the side of the road. He thought, "I won't listen to my ma, I'll save money and build my house of straw." He began building his house of straw.

"I'll build my house of straw and it is going to be fine.

And when I'm done building, this house will be all mine."

Now the second little pig saw a stick seller by the side of the road. He thought, "Better to be cheap and quick, I'll save money and build my house of sticks." He began building his house of sticks.

"I'll build my house of sticks and it is going to be fine.

And when I'm done building, this house will be all mine."

Now the oldest pig, he was smart and remembered his mama's wise words. He said, "Brick costs more but it sure is strong and I know it will make the house last long!" So he bought bricks.

"I'm gonna build my house of bricks and it is gonna be fine.

And when I'm done building, this house will be all mine."

Meanwhile, the big bad wolf smelled something tasty. He smelled bacon! The big bad wolf went to house of straw and knocked on the door.

"Hey Little Pig, Hey Little Pig!

Won't you let me come in?"

97

"No!" said the pig, "No!" said the pig.

"Not by the hair of my chinny chin chin."

"Then I'll huff," said the wolf,

"And I'll puff," said the wolf,

"And I will blow your house down."

So he huffed, yes he did.

And he puffed, yes he did.

And he blew (whoosh) the house down!

The first little pig squealed, "Wee, wee, wee!" all the way to the home of the second little pig. But the wolf followed. The big bad wolf went to the house of straw and knocked on the door.

"Hey Little Pigs, Hey Little Pigs!

Won't you let me come in?"

"No!" said the pigs, "No!" said the pigs.

"Not by the hair of our chinny chin chin."

"Then I'll huff," said the wolf,

"And I'll puff," said the wolf,

"And I will blow your house down."

So he huffed, yes he did.

And he puffed, yes he did.

And he blew (whoosh) the house down!

The two little pigs squealed, "Wee, wee, wee!" all the way to the home of their big brother. Now the third little pig knew the big bad wolf would come sooner or later. But he was sure that his house of bricks was tough and strong.

Sure enough, the wolf followed. The big bad wolf thought, "Boy, am I going to have some fun. I get three little pigs for the price of one!" The big bad wolf went to the house of bricks and knocked on the door.

"Hey Little Pigs, Hey Little Pigs!

Won't you let me come in?"

"No!" said the pigs, "No!" said the pigs.

"Not by the hair of our chinny chin chin."

"Then I'll huff," said the wolf,

"And I'll puff," said the wolf,

"And I will blow your house down."

So he huffed, yes he did.

And he puffed, yes he did.

And he blew (whoosh)

And he blew (whoosh)

And he blew!

But the house didn't come down.

The wolf was pretty upset. He was VERY hungry and determined! He climbed onto the roof and began sliding down the chimney!

Now, as I told you before, the third little pig was the wise one. As soon as he heard the wolf scrambling above, he placed a pot of water in the fireplace. It bubbled and it boiled. When the wolf came down, he found himself . . . in hot water! The wolf fell in, much to his chagrin. And the three little pigs were never bothered again.

Whose afraid of the big bad wolf? The big bad wolf. The big bad wolf.

Whose afraid of the big bad wolf?

Tra la la la la la la

We're not afraid of the big bad wolf! The big bad wolf. The big bad wolf.

We're not afraid of the big bad wolf!

Tra la la la la la la

The Tortoise and the Hare

Aesop Fable from Greece

From a far off land neither here nor there

I bring you the fable of the Tortoise and the Hare.

Hare was very conceited and thought that he was the most handsome animal in all the forest. He would often gaze into the mirror and say, "I am so handsome. Look at my lovely long ears, my pretty pink nose, and my beautiful buck teeth!" He also thought that he was the fastest animal in all the forest.

One day, Hare overheard a group of turtles talking. They said, "Cousin Tortoise has never lost a race. He always wins!"

"Ha!" scoffed Hare, "We'll see about that!" He marched over to the group of turtles and said, "Everyone knows that I am the fastest animal in all the forest. Tell your cousin Tortoise that I challenge him to a race!"

The next day, Tortoise met Hare in the clearing. He said, "Hello, I am Tortoise. Are you ready to race?"

Hare answered with a laugh, "Of course I am because I am the fastest animal in all the forest. Prepare to eat my dust!"

Tortoise and Hare lined up. Raccoon held her tail up in the air and said, "On your mark, ready, ready, go!"

Hare took off and left Tortoise in a cloud of dust. Meanwhile . . .

Tortoise never wavered from the race.

He kept on going at a steady pace.

Hare looked behind and saw that he was far ahead of Tortoise. He decided he had time for a little break. So he stopped by the side of the road and pulled out his mirror.

101

He said, "Just look at me. So handsome. Not a hair out of place." As Hare admired himself, he saw another reflection in the mirror. It was . . . Tortoise! You see . . .

Tortoise never wavered from the race.

He kept on going at a steady pace.

Hare yelled, "Oh no! I gotta go!" And he took off faster than a speeding bullet. Hare looked behind and saw that he was way ahead of Tortoise. He decided that he had time for a little snack, so he decided to stop and eat. He was munching and crunching when he saw . . . Tortoise! You see . . .

Tortoise never wavered from the race.

He kept on going at a steady pace.

Hare yelled, "Oh no! I gotta go!" and he took off faster than a tornado. Hare ran for a while. Then he looked behind and saw that he was way, way ahead of Tortoise. There was no sign of Tortoise at all! Hare decided that he had time for a little . . . nap. He sat down by the side of the road, under the shade of a tall tree, and began to snooze. (snoring sounds) Meanwhile . . .

Tortoise never wavered from the race.

He kept on going at a steady pace.

Hare woke up just in time to see Tortoise approaching the finish line. Hare yelled, "Oh no! I gotta go!" and he took off faster than lightning. But it was too late. Although Hare was close behind, Tortoise crossed the finish line. Tortoise won the race by just a . . . hare! You see . . .

Tortoise never wavered from the race.

He kept on going at a steady pace.

Source Notes

"Anansi's Hat Shaking Dance" was adapted from "Anansi's Hat-Shaking Dance" in *The Arbuthnot Anthology of Children's Literature, Third Edition,* edited by May Hill Arbuthnot (Glenview, IL: Scott, Foresman and Company, 1952) and "Anansi's Hat-shaking Dance" in *Best-Loved Folktales of the World,* edited by Joanna Cole (New York: Anchor Books, 1982).

"Ant and the Grasshopper, The" was adapted from "The Ants and the Grasshopper" in *Aesop's Fables,* selected and adapted by Jack Zipes (New York: The Penguin Group, 1992), "The Ants and the Grasshopper" in *The Aesop for Children* (New York: Scholastic, 1994) and "The Ant and the Grasshopper" in *The Arbuthnot Anthology of Children's Literature, Third Edition,* edited by May Hill Arbuthnot (Glenview, IL: Scott, Foresman and Company, 1961).

"Beauty and the Beast" was adapted from "Beauty and the Beast" in *The Blue Fairy Book,* edited by Andrew Lang (New York: MJF Books, 1889), "Beauty and the Beast" in *Best-Loved Folktales of the World,* edited by Joanna Cole (New York: Anchor Books, 1982), and "Beauty and the Beast" in *The Everything Fairy Tales Book* by Amy Peters (Avon, MA: Adams Media Corporation, 2001).

"Brer Rabbit and the Tar Baby" was adapted from "The Wonderful Tar Baby Story" in *A Treasury of American Folklore,* edited by B. A. Botkin (New York: Crown Publishers, 1944), "Brer Rabbit and the Tar Baby" in *The Tales of Uncle Remus: The Adventures of Brer Rabbit,* as told by Julius Lester (New York: Dial Books, 1987). "Brer Fox, Brer Rabbit, and the Tar-Baby" in *The Classic Tales of Brer Rabbit,* retold by David Borgenicht from stories collected by Joel Chandler Harris (Philadelphia, PA: Courage Books, 1995) and "The Wonderful Tar-Baby Story" in *Best-Loved Folktales of the World,* edited by Joanna Cole (New York: Anchor Books, 1982).

"Briar Rose (Sleeping Beauty)" was adapted from "The Sleeping Beauty in the Wood" in *The Blue Fairy Book,* edited by Andrew Lang (New York: MJF Books, 1889), "Briar Rose" in *Classic Library Folktales: The Brothers Grimm* (New York: Anness Publishing, Limited, 1995, originally published in 1870) and "Sleeping Beauty" in *Best-Loved Folktales of the World,* edited by Joanna Cole (New York: Anchor Books, 1982).

"Cinderella" was adapted from "Cinderella" in *The Blue Fairy Book,* edited by Andrew Lang (New York: MJF Books, 1889), "Cinderella" in *Classic Library Folktales: The Brothers Grimm* (New York: Anness Publishing, Limited, 1995, originally published in 1870) and "Cinderella" in *Best-Loved Folktales of the World,* edited by Joanna Cole (New York: Anchor Books, 1982).

"Frog Prince, The" was adapted from "The Frog Prince" in *Classic Library Folktales: The Brothers Grimm* (New York: Anness Publishing, Limited, 1995, originally published in 1870), "The

Frog Prince" in *Best-Loved Folktales of the World*, edited by Joanna Cole (New York: Anchor Books by Doubleday, 1982) and "The Frog Prince" in *The Everything Fairy Tales Book* by Amy Peters (Avon, MA: Adams Media Corporation, 2001).

"Gingerbread Man, The" was adapted from childhood memories of the story, "Journey Cake, Ho!" in *The Arbuthnot Anthology of Children's Literature, Third Edition*, edited by May Hill Arbuthnot (Glenview, IL: Scott, Foresman and Company, 1961), "Johnnycake" in *The Everything Fairy Tales Book* by Amy Peters (Avon, MA: Adams Media Corporation, 2001), and "The Pancake" in *The Arbuthnot Anthology of Children's Literature, Third Edition*, edited by May Hill Arbuthnot (Glenview, IL: Scott, Foresman and Company, 1961).

"Goldie Locks and the Three Bears" was adapted from "The Story of Pretty Goldilocks" in *The Blue Fairy Book*, edited by Andrew Lang (New York: MJF Books, 1889), "The Story of the Three Bears" in *English Fairy Tales* by Joseph Jacobs (New York: Alfred A. Knopf, 1993, first published in 1890), and "The Story of the Three Bears" in *The Arbuthnot Anthology of Children's Literature, Third Edition*, edited by May Hill Arbuthnot (Glenview, IL: Scott, Foresman and Company, 1961).

"Hansel and Gretel" was adapted from "Hansel and Grettel" in *The Blue Fairy Book*, edited by Andrew Lang (New York: MJF Books, 1889), "Hansel and Grethel" in *Classic Library Folktales: The Brothers Grimm* (New York: Anness Publishing, Limited, 1995, originally published in 1870) and "Hansel and Gretel" in *Best-Loved Folktales of the World*, edited by Joanna Cole (New York: Anchor Books, 1982).

"Henny Penny" was adapted from "Henny Penny" in *English Fairy Tales* by Joseph Jacobs (New York: Alfred A. Knopf, 1993, first published in 1890), "Henny-Penny" in *The Arbuthnot Anthology of Children's Literature, Third Edition*, edited by May Hill Arbuthnot (Glenview, IL: Scott, Foresman and Company, 1961) and "Henny-Penny" in *The Everything Fairy Tales Book* by Amy Peters (Avon, MA: Adams Media Corporation, 2001).

"Jack and the Beanstalk" was adapted from "Jack and the Beanstalk" in *The Red Fairy Book*, edited by Andrew Lang (New York: MFJ Books, 1994, originally published in 1890), "Jack and the Beanstalk" in *Best-Loved Folktales of the World*, edited by Joanna Cole (New York: Anchor Books by Doubleday, 1982) and "Jack and the Beanstalk" in *English Fairy Tales* by Joseph Jacobs (New York: Alfred A. Knopf, 1993, first published in 1890).

"Jack Seeks His Fortune" was adapted from "How Jack Went to Seek His Fortune" in *Troll Treasury of Animal Stories*, edited by John C. Miles (Mahwah, NJ: Harper Collins, 1991), "Jack and the Robbers" in *The Jack Tales* by Ray Hicks (New York: Callaway, 2000) and "How Jack Went to Seek His Fortune" in *English Fairy Tales* by Joseph Jacobs (New York: Alfred A. Knopf, 1993, first published in 1890).

"Lion and the Mouse, The" was adapted from childhood memories of the story "The Lion and the Mouse" in *Aesop's Fables*, selected and adapted by Jack Zipes (New York: The Penguin Group, 1992), "The Lion and the Mouse" in *The Aesop for Children* (New York: Scholastic, 1994), and "The Lion and the Mouse" in *The Arbuthnot Anthology of Children's Literature, Third Edition*, edited by May Hill Arbuthnot (Glenview, IL: Scott, Foresman and Company, 1961).

"Little Red Hen, The" was adapted from childhood memories of the story, "The Little Red Hen and the Grain of Wheat" in *Story Time of My Bookhouse*, edited by Olive Beaupré Miller (Lake Bluff, IL: The Book House for Children, 1965) and "Little Red Hen and the Grains of Wheat" in *Troll Treasury of Animal Stories*, edited by John C. Miles (Mahwah, NJ: Harper Collins, 1991).

"Little Red Riding Hood" was adapted from "The Little Red Riding Hood" in *The Blue Fairy Book*, edited by Andrew Lang (New York: MJF Books, 1889), "Little Red Riding Hood" in *Best-Loved Folktales of the World*, edited by Joanna Cole (New York: Anchor Books, 1982) and "Little Red Riding Hood" in *The Everything Fairy Tales Book* by Amy Peters (Avon, MA: Adams Media Corporation, 2001).

"Natasha and Baba Yaga" was adapted from "The Baba Yaga" in *Best-Loved Folktales of the World*, edited by Joanna Cole (New York: Anchor Books by Doubleday, 1982) and "Bony Legs" in *The Scary Book*, edited by Joanna Cole and Stephanie Calmenson (New York: Doubleday Books, 1991).

"Paul Bunyan and the Great Popcorn Blizzard" was adapted from "The Popcorn Blizzard" in *Paul Bunyan Swings His Axe* by Dell J. McCormick (Caldwell, ID: The Caxton Printers, Ltd., 1962) and "Paul's Popcorn" in *A Treasury of North American Folktales*, compiled by Catherine Peck (New York: The Philip Lief Group, 1998).

"Pecos Bill" was adapted from *Pecos Bill* by Nanci A. Lyman (Mahweh, NJ: Troll Associates, 1980), "The Saga of Pecos Bill" in *A Treasury of American Folklore*, edited by B. A. Botkin (New York: Crown Publishers, 1944) and "Ride 'em, Round' em, Rope 'em: The Story of Pecos Bill" retold by Brian Gleeson in *From Sea to Shining Sea*, compiled by Amy L. Cohn (New York: Scholastic, 1993).

"Princess and the Bean, The" was adapted from "The Princess on the Bean" in *Classic Library Fairytales: Hans Christian Andersen* (New York: Anness Publishing, Limited, 1995, originally published in 1872), "The Princess on the Pea" in *The Complete Fairy Tales and Stories: Hans Christian Andersen* (New York: Barnes & Noble, and Worth Press, Ltd., 2007) and "The Princess and the Pea" in *The Everything Fairy Tales Book* by Amy Peters (Avon, MA: Adams Media Corporation, 2001).

"Rapunzel" was adapted from "Rapunzel" in *Classic Library Folktales: The Brothers Grimm* (New York: Anness Publishing, Limited, 1995, originally published in 1870), "Rapunzel" in *The Red Fairy Book*, edited by Andrew Lang (New York: MFJ Books, 1994, originally published in 1890), "Rapunzel" in *Best-Loved Folktales of the World*, edited by Joanna Cole (New York: Anchor Books by Doubleday, 1982) and "Rapunzel" in *The Everything Fairy Tales Book* by Amy Peters (Avon, MA: Adams Media Corporation, 2001).

"Sody Sallyraytus" was adapted from "Sody Sallyraytus" in *Grandfather Tales*, collected and retold by Richard Chase (Cambridge, MA: The Riverside Press, 1948) and "Sody Saleratus" in *Crocodile! Crocodile! Stories Told Around the World* by Barbara Baumgartner (New York: Dorling Kindersley Publishing, 1994).

"Three Billy Goats Gruff, The" was adapted from "The Three Billygoats Gruff" in *Best-Loved Folktales of the World*, edited by Joanna Cole (New York: Anchor Books, 1982), "The Three

Billy-Goats Gruff" in *The Arbuthnot Anthology of Children's Literature, Third Edition*, edited by May Hill Arbuthnot (Glenview, IL: Scott, Foresman and Company, 1961) and "The Three Billy Goats Gruff" in *The Everything Fairy Tales Book* by Amy Peters (Avon, MA: Adams Media Corporation, 2001).

"Three Little Pigs, The" was adapted from "The Story of the Three Little Pigs" in *English Fairy Tales* by Joseph Jacobs (New York: Alfred A. Knopf, 1993, first published in 1890) and "The Story of the Three Little Pigs" in *The Arbuthnot Anthology of Children's Literature, Third Edition*, edited by May Hill Arbuthnot (Glenview, IL: Scott, Foresman and Company, 1961).

"Tortoise and the Hare, The" was adapted from childhood memories of the story "The Hare and the Tortoise" in *Aesop's Fables*, selected and adapted by Jack Zipes (New York: The Penguin Group, 1992), "The Tortoise and the Hare" in *Troll Treasury of Animal Stories*, edited by John C. Miles (Mahwah, NJ: Harper Collins, 1991) and "The Hare and the Tortoise" in *Best-Loved Folktales of the World*, edited by Joanna Cole (New York: Anchor Books, 1982).

About the Author and Illustrator

DIANNE DE LAS CASAS is an author and award-winning storyteller who tours internationally presenting programs, educator/librarian training, workshops, and artist residencies. Her performances, dubbed "traditional folklore gone fun" and "revved-up storytelling," are full of energetic audience participation. Dianne's professional books include *Story Fest: Crafting Story Theater Scripts*; *Kamishibai Story Theater: The Art of Picture Telling*; *Handmade Tales: Stories to Make and Take*; *Tangram Tales: Story Theater Using the Ancient Chinese Puzzle*, *The Story Biz Handbook*, and *Scared Silly: 25 Tales to Tickle and Thrill*. Her children's books include *The Cajun Cornbread Boy, Madame Poulet & Monsieur Roach*, and *Mama's Bayou*. Visit her website at www.storyconnection.net.

SOLEIL LISETTE is a graphic design student at Louisiana State University in Baton Rouge. Since she was two years old, she could always be found with a pen in her hand—drawing! Her career aspirations include illustrating children's books and beginning her own line of cosmetics. When not at school, Soleil lives in the New Orleans area. Visit Soleil's website at www.soleil-lisette.com.